broke but unbroken

broke but unbroken

Grassroots Social Movements
and Their Radical Solutions
to Poverty

augusta dwyer

Fernwood Publishing • Halifax & Winnipeg
Kumarian Press • Sterling, VA

Editing and design: Brenda Conroy
Cover design: John van der Woude
Printed and bound in Canada by Hignell Book Printing

Published in Canada by Fernwood Publishing
32 Oceanvista Lane, Black Point, Nova Scotia, B0J 1B0
and 748 Broadway Avenue, Winnipeg, MB R3G 0X3   www.fernwoodpublishing.ca
and in the United States by Kumarian Press
22883 Quicksilver Drive, Sterling, VA 20166-2012   www.kpbooks.com

Fernwood Publishing Company Limited gratefully acknowledges the financial support of the
Government of Canada through the Canada Book Fund, the Canada Council for the Arts,
the Nova Scotia Department of Tourism and Culture, the Manitoba Department of Culture,
Heritage and Tourism under the Manitoba Publishers Marketing Assistance Program and the
Province of Manitoba, through the Book Publishing Tax Credit, for our publishing program.

Library and Archives Canada Cataloguing in Publication

Dwyer, Augusta
Broke but unbroken: grassroots social movements and their radical solutions to poverty /
Augusta Dwyer.

Includes bibliographical references and index.
ISBN 978-1-55266-406-3

1. Social movements. 2. Poor—Political activity. 3. Economic assistance, Domestic. I. Title.

HM881.D99 2011   362.5'7   C2010-908030-0

Library of Congress Cataloging-in-Publication Data

Dwyer, Augusta, 1956-
Broke but unbroken : grassroots social movements and their radical
solutions to poverty / Augusta Dwyer.
p. cm.
Includes bibliographical references and index.
ISBN 978-1-56549-447-3 (pbk. : alk. paper) -- ISBN 978-1-56549-448-0
(library ebook) -- ISBN 978-1-56549-449-7 (consumer ebook)
1. Social movements--Developing countries. 2. Voluntarism--Developing
countries. I. Title.
HM881.D994 2011   303.48'4091724--dc22   2011008712

Contents

Introduction

Dealing with Hope

It is not through resignation but resistance in the face of injustice that we affirm ourselves as human beings. — Paulo Freire

Near the corner where First Road meets a traffic circle called Alankar Chowk, a group of cart pullers wait for work, playing cards or resting from the effort of hauling heavy loads throughout the city of Mumbai. Below a small shrine tiled with the image of a kindly white-bearded man in an orange robe, their narrow wooden handcarts are parked side by side like skiffs in a harbour. The *chowk* — which in Hindi means "a place where paths intersect" — is hemmed in by rundown apartment buildings, dilapidated little shops and small businesses like the one that announces, unabashedly, "Portfolio Management." The *chowk* swells and blares with a seemingly constant flow of traffic, of taxis, trucks and cars. From sidewalk booths, ribbons of lottery tickets and multicoloured packets of tobacco waft in the fumes of all those combustion engines engulfing the hot afternoon breeze.

Pedestrians, bicycles and men pulling handcarts loaded with odd yet practical items — worn-out air conditioners, huge piles of burlap, a dozen rolls of metal sheeting — make their way through the traffic. Along the mostly broken sidewalk, the fruit vendors burn sticks of incense among their wares and women string loops of marigold and jasmine to sell to the crowds of passers-by. Men and women alike load sacks and boxes onto their heads or curl up in the shade of a wall, somehow managing to find the oblivion of sleep within this vast grid of commercial activity.

This snapshot of a chaotic, busy intersection where the poor come to work, to sell or to beg is real, and replicated in underdeveloped countries around the world. Yet it is also emblematic of the way many people, including policymakers, the media and even philanthropists, tend to see the poor and poverty: as a problem so vast and so complicated that the poor themselves could not possibly have any solutions to bring to it. They are victims, not protagonists, lacking the time, the tools and the desire to think about the politics of their situation. For many, the slum dweller and the impoverished peasant farmer are not like the rest of us somehow. Even in wealthy nations, the poor are seen as risk-averse, as incapable of long-term planning, as individuals scrambling to make ends meet on their own without any real sense of collectivism or political agency. Thus, poverty is to be survived by the poor, and solved by those who are not.

However, Alankar Chowk is also a place where paths of perception intersect. "Cities, especially but by no means exclusively those in the developing world," writes South African political scientist Mark Swilling, "are now locales of hopelessness and hope: hopelessness due to the sheer magnitude of the challenges we face, and hope due to the efforts of countless social movements that are finding ingenious solutions to intractable problems in the complex interstices of these awesome, unsustainable social structures." This book deals with the hope. In fact, it goes beyond hope to look at the actual achievements of four grassroots social movements of the poor. It shows how, in their quest for rights and resources, they are proving to be far more successful than traditional aid initiatives, progressively minded governments or piecemeal economic growth in ameliorating the conditions of poverty. Among these organizations is the Indian Alliance, which has an office on First Road. Originally formed in 1976 as the Bombay Slum Dwellers Federation, the Alliance today unites some two million slum and pavement dwellers. Their struggle for housing and tenure rights is just one example of how, increasingly, poor people are recognizing that they do not have to accept the bondage of poverty. Their achievements in changing not only the circumstances to which fate seems to have destined them to live their lives, but also traditional perceptions of them as helpless recipients of aid, are bringing an entirely new focus to the poverty debate.

Over the past several decades, particular global tendencies have exacerbated the growth of Third World poverty. These are the seemingly bland and anodyne features that by now constitute the reigning capitalist orthodoxy. Its features include the exploitation of resources for the benefit of large, international corporations, the constant search for new trade niches and ever-cheaper labour, and the blatant promotion of agribusiness and its addiction to chemicals. Throw in the fiscal policies imposed by global bodies such as the International Monetary Fund and the World Trade Organization on debtor nations, and you have a continuous assault on the lives of poor and indigenous peoples, a big, relentless and efficient system for poverty growth. As Swilling sums it up, "the power of those who control the world's resources depends on the systemic disempowerment of the global poor."

Yet alleviating economic and social inequality is also, by and large, determined by those at the top. In the predominant view of both government leaders and society in general, the only way to eradicate poverty is with some of our rich-nation money — an idea that evolved from a previous belief that what the poor needed was to be civilized. With no way of making a connection to the cart pullers or beggars or street vendors, society trusts its governments and international institutions to do so — to deliver the sacks of grain, the vaccinations, the multi-million-dollar advice that will fortify capitalism, create jobs and change lives.

Another popular view has to do with the reforming powers of progressive politics. If the poor were to elect the right party to government, it would be accountable to the people. Development would blossom, equality reign and poverty slowly disappear, just like their candidates always promise. For others, effective government would also allow the market to function as it apparently should. Private enterprise, modernized and unfettered, would create the wealth and jobs that will eventually lift the poor from poverty, like a giant tidal wave of economic energy.

Yet for all the donations, foundations, soft loans, debt forgiveness and development schemes, the spectre of poverty only seems to proliferate. We have only to look at countries like Brazil or South Africa for just a couple of examples of political parties within which the aspirations of the poor and oppressed coalesced, that once elected, ignored their discourse, their promises and even their history. In developing nations such as India, Brazil and Indonesia, sustained growth of gross domestic product (GDP) has failed to bring the prosperity the market promises to billions of people. India's astoundingly high childhood malnutrition rates, for example, have barely moved, from 42.7 percent in 1999 to 40.4 percent in 2006 — despite the economic growth of those years. Even the concerted might of the United Nations and its famous Millennium Development Goals (MDGs) have brought only piecemeal improvements, while their main target — to halve extreme poverty by 2015 — seems as distant as it did in 2000, when the initiative was declared and signed.

Today, about half of the world population — almost three billion people — live in poverty: in refugee camps, in city slums and in an increasingly ungiving countryside that is still home to something like three quarters of the global poor. An extraordinary number of them, 800 million, are chronically hungry and malnourished. In Africa, half the population still lives on $1 a day, and almost half — 42 percent — do not even have access to clean drinking water. Meanwhile, global warming and environmental destruction are making small-scale farming an ever more unviable proposition. Overwhelmed by the media images of the world we share with the poor, it is no wonder people in rich nations believe the message that poverty is so complex that only an elite layer of experts, policymakers, corporations and economists can eventually figure out some mechanism to end it.

However, the grassroots social movements increasingly shouldering their way onto the world stage defy that belief as they seek a world far different in social and economic terms than the one we live in now. They understand that it is their right *not* to be landless, homeless or unemployed while national and international economic policies favour a few and disregard the rest. The millions of poor people who form and run these movements show that beyond those dismal scenes of Third World poverty, behind the multiple realities of economic injustice, something significant is going on, as momentous to the rest of us as it is to the poor themselves. How and why they organize, the way they struggle for more than mere survival, but for rights, education and social justice, not only challenge the decision-making hegemony of national governments and global institutions, they also question long-held assumptions about what the poor can and want to achieve, not only for themselves but for entire societies.

The terms "grassroots" and "social movements" are broad and fluid concepts nowadays, taking in everything from professional organizations that work among the poor, to community-based organizations, to protest mobilizations. Recent history has brought us Yellow, Orange and Velvet revolutions as examples of "people power," as well as civil rights, women's and environmental movements, groups of unrepresented or disenfranchised members of affluent societies who fell outside standard class analysis.

The movements whose stories are related in this book are all based in low-income or underdeveloped countries. They are made up of impoverished people who have joined together to struggle for some concrete goal along with other enduring, often intangible goals that arise as a result of these same struggles. Their aims are both immediate and long-term. They encompass each participant's desire for land, housing or jobs, as well as empowerment and eventual social change. These movements therefore combine elements of protest and resistance with the kinds of activities carried out typically by non-governmental organizations, or NGOs, activities that involve the ongoing search for sustainable solutions in the lives of the poor. This dual nature gives them undeniable staying power and is a major factor in their achievements in fighting poverty.

Swilling, who heads the Sustainability Institute at the University of Stellenbosch in South Africa, sees the work of such movements as building "self-organized systems within poor communities." He notes the way they remain autonomous whether they are engaged in conflicts or negotiations, or in partnership with other bodies such as local governments and development agencies. "What changes when this happens," he points out, "is not the power relations per se but rather the way solutions are defined, contested, negotiated and implemented. Over time, the substance of these power relationships starts to change."

Grassroots social movements that have over the years proven themselves successful in achieving such solutions — essentially in their struggles against poverty and exclusion — are the focus of this book. Three of them, the Indian Alliance, the Peasant Union of Indonesia and Brazil's Landless Rural Workers Movement, have amassed remarkably large memberships over several decades. The fourth, the National Movement of Factories Recovered by Workers, is comparatively small, with some 10,000 members, and still relatively new. The social and historical implications of its success in taking over and running 122 workplaces in Argentina since 2001, however, convinced me that this organization needed to be included. It is a phenomenon that, as City University of New York political scientist Peter Ranis noted in *Socialism and Democracy*, "reinserts the working class as a central ingredient in the pursuit of a just society."

I followed other criteria as well, choosing to concentrate on movements that had been initiated essentially by the poor themselves and that promote participatory democracy within their structures. Extraordinarily heartening in and of itself, I believe this respect for the opinions and decisions of every member is a key feature of these movements' success and potential. It explains the broadening of the issues they are taking on beyond the original or basic demands, such as, in the case of the Landless Rural Workers Movement, meaningful education as well as a plot of land. Taken together, these features shed new light on the way millions of the planet's most disadvantaged people think about, care about and set about consciously building structures of democracy, responsibility and justice.

While resistance to a system that denies them access to resources lies at their core, they have proven to be more resilient than many straightforward opposition movements. Mobilization may begin over a single problematic issue or particular crisis, yet as this is overcome, members remain in the movement and retain the features of protest, such as demonstrations, occupations and other forms of direct action. A common language of rights allows them to embrace specific demands but also contributes to alliances with others in diverse countries, cultures and contexts.

This broadening of the parameters of struggle and defining of solutions to poverty imply a significant evolution of the protest movement. The slum dwellers in the Indian Alliance, for example, identify land on which housing for them may be built. In a context where water and electricity often fail, they design and oversee construction of the housing in order to make sure it works for them; invariably, it ends up costing much less than had it been built by the state or an international institution. In Brazil, the Landless Rural Workers Movement, or MST, promotes the setting up of cooperatives, organic farming and responsible use of the environment among its members to help them compete with large landowners and agribusiness.

Scholars of social movements have long attempted to define their inner workings and the historical circumstances surrounding their formation.

They consider, for example, the rational calculations individuals must make in order to join a social or solidarity movement; in other words, how it has to be in their interest as individuals to do so. Some, like University of Florida anthropologist Anthony Oliver-Smith in his study of resistance movements to big development projects, also consider other factors, what he calls "the bonds of sentiment, affect and other *gemeinshaft* emotions in the formation of solidarity groups." Oliver–Smith identifies the tension between these ideas as "one of the most persistent issues in social movement research," and observes how "certain kinds of movements based on concepts of collective identity, spiritual values, or aesthetics… can be dismissed as patently irrational and given short shrift by policy-makers and other authorities."

While such scrutiny is not the focus of this book, what is interesting in the movements studied here is the combination of both the rational and the "emotional." Those joining or forming the social movement make concrete gains. But at the same time we find identification with the movement, internal diversity and the adoption of meaningful rituals — such as the political theatricals, or *misticas*, devised by the MST in Brazil — as a kind of emotional or ideological hook. Just as the personal experiences and perceptions of participants are multiple, fluid and often a question of process, they absorb and exchange meanings among themselves and with their coordinators in understanding their situation. A powerful sense of identification with the movement and its long-term goals allows them to keep growing, in size and relevance, as members take on more and more of the multiple problems that confront them.

The importance each of the four social movements described in the following chapters places on participatory democracy is particularly noteworthy, inspiring and instructive. To what extent does the requirement some see for articulate and even charismatic leaders in determining the success of social movements find balance with a need for such participatory democracy within them? This question is also linked to the notion of "framing," as originated by Canadian sociologist Erving Goffman in 1974. Goffman came up with the concept of framing to describe the set of interpretations individuals use to perceive their reality and from that, guide their actions. Frame "alignment" is seen as the main role of movement leaders, as they articulate the need to change the predominant social view that poverty is the fault of the poor (or in some cases, previous colonizers) rather than an inevitable ingredient of capitalism. The experiences of the grassroots movements described in this book provide intriguing examples of how to find and support just such a balance.

Although the role of leaders in the Indian Alliance, for example, has been crucial to its success, the frame they provide is their emphasis on the reality that slum and street dwellers, by simply surviving, have amassed a huge amount of skills and knowledge usually taken for granted. What's more, as this movement spreads from Mumbai to cities across India, knowledge is transmitted by and amongst its members rather than by outside development experts or social workers. The balance here is also between individual responsibility and empowerment, and this makes the Alliance's critique of traditional national and international development methods both pointed and constructive.

In Argentina, horizontal decision-making is the basis of every cooperative determined to keep its source of employment by taking over and running its workplace. The recuperation of moribund factories by workers occurred against the backdrop of a crashing economy, stratospheric rates of unemployment and a resulting poverty boom. As business owners simply walked away from their companies (many of which had enjoyed hefty subsidies from the Argentine taxpayer), some workers decided to stay and run things themselves. Out of the massive street protests and generalized anger against a system that clearly wasn't functioning, the National Movement of Factories Recovered by Workers, or MNFRT, has emerged as the leading organization representing the cooperative self-management of workplaces in all kinds of sectors. In every member cooperative, decisions are taken through workers' assemblies. Elected factory councils can be recalled at any time if they don't carry out their responsibilities, and profits are equally divided among cooperative members. While in some cases, such democracy has been challenged by leftwing political parties seeking to utilize them as an example, or even by their own factory councils intent on lining their pockets, the power of the majority has always won out. The economic transparency of the cooperative makes every single worker-managed workplace a success story in itself, a microcosm of workers' power and collective strength.

In the case of the Peasant Union of Indonesia, or SPI, the equilibrium between decentralized decision-making and the ability to speak in a unified voice is fundamental to both its internal democracy and its success. Its early years were characterized by a series of isolated or regional responses to land theft and repression by corporations and government during the authoritarian, thirty-two-year-long regime of Suharto. At the time, the creation of a national organization whose aim was to forcibly take fertile farmland would have been illegal, even as activists recognized that just such a movement was needed. Only with the post-Suharto Reformasi, or Reform, did open organizing become possible, allowing the SPI to grow to a membership of 700,000 smallholders and forest dwellers. As they exchange ideas, information and decisions among themselves and with a central office in Jakarta, many thousands of twenty-five-member bases across the vast Indonesian archipelago now sustain the values of autonomy.

In its struggle to win back or retain the rights of Indonesia's forest peasants, moreover, the SPI is promoting another kind of democracy, environmental democracy. The state's control of millions of hectares of land through the creation of a national forest puts them at the centre of most agrarian struggles in Indonesia today. Throughout Southeast Asia, in fact, an astonishingly high number of peasants — more than 100 million — live in forests. Powerful interests in logging, mining and agribusiness leave most of them subject to eviction at any time. And one of the latest schemes to fight global warming, Reduced Emissions from Deforestation and Forest Degradation, will, ironically, exacerbate the precarious nature of their tenure. The SPI's rights-based approach to environmental conservation, therefore, comes into direct conflict with the notion that preserving tropical forests means cutting the people who live in them out of the equation. As such, it has enormous repercussions for the entire region.

In Brazil, the MST consciously discards the notion of hierarchical leadership for what one militant describes as "circles of representation," continually training new leaders and recycling old ones throughout the entire organization. When it began in the late 1970s, its members were encouraged, championed and even protected by churches and left-leaning trade unionists. Yet those who stood on the front lines were the destitute peasants evicted from large estates by the switch to mechanized farming. Those who occupied the first pieces of public lands and demanded their expropriation for their own use, lived for years in black tarp shacks and direct the movement today are the landless peasants themselves.

This is not to say that in these and in other examples of grassroots movements, those who are not poor — sympathetic outsiders in a sense — cannot or do not play important roles. At issue is the potential for tension, for the movement being taken over by supporters or organizers who may well be capable of articulating a deeper, more structural dimension to what is otherwise a series of personal tribulations. As Srilatha Batliwala of the Hauser Center for Nonprofit Organizations at Harvard University has observed, "This broadening of the term grassroots and grassroots movements disguises the very real difference in power, resources, visibility, access, structure, ideology and strategies between movements of directly affected people and those of their champions, spokespeople or advocates." The price of information, technology, experience and even financial support can be high, from internal strife to meddling with the decision-making processes of the majority. In the most successful grassroots social movements, this potential imbalance is replaced with alliance, with mutual learning and with a deep respect for autonomy. There is a recognition that while cross-class solidarity can be a significant moral and ideological lever for those forced by the dominating class to feel like nonentities in their own society, it must encourage rather than stifle their voices and sense of initiative.

After twenty years in the MST, for example, a former Catholic lay worker named Rubinilsa Leandro de Souza still remembers how she felt, setting out in the middle of the night, during the first fitful land occupations in Pernambuco. "People are believing in you," she said, "in you, this young person. You jump up into the truck and head for the land, and when you arrive, there are another 400 families. And so you begin to believe in the average person's strength, to feel that, when the people are organized, they have invincible strength. I think that is what motivates you, what makes you believe — the fact that you actually have a concrete proposal for a particular situation."

Rubinilsa's experiences led her to drop her lay work for the church and dedicate herself fulltime to the MST, compelled, as she put it, by "this desire to see something being done that transformed people." In fact, the diverse personal stories related in the following chapters portray this transformation. They are just a few of the multiple examples of how participation in collective struggles brings the most disadvantaged and marginalized of people to take on, in a personal sense, bigger questions about the nature of social justice and democracy. No one comes out of a struggle the same person they went in. Experiences of repression and solidarity unearth inner resources and strength of purpose many didn't know they possessed. The overcoming of obstacles leads to the discovery of a new consciousness and confidence. Like a snake discarding its old skin, the poor who construct change at the same time shed the culturally embedded belief that only small groups of elite decision-makers know what is best for them.

The experience of struggle can also provide fertile ground for the blossoming of the creativity of the poor. In the district of Pandeglang, on the Indonesian island of Java, Saeful Anwar makes his living from a single hectare of land. This he carefully terraces and tills, hand planting rice twice a year, planting cassava and fruit trees along its margins. Regularly flooding and filling his plot with goldfish bring three undeniable advantages: natural fertilizer, pest control and, eventually, dinner. Yet Saeful represents far more than the industrious peasant farmer in a lush landscape of glimmering steppes of water and emerald carpets of young rice. He is also an example of the inventiveness, optimism and altruism of the poor. He promotes the use of organic fertilizers among local peasant farmers and, after gathering information from the elders in his village, has concocted an organic pesticide. He has even invented a simple system for pumping water up from lower fields to higher ones, three pipes and a faucet that cost a few dollars to buy and don't need a motor to work. This invention, too, he wants to give away to other peasants like himself. The fact that he doesn't do this as just an individual, but as a member of a thriving social movement, is what lends him and his inventiveness heightened relevance in the global struggle for economic and social justice. Saeful joined the SPI, he said, "because I felt that the rights of peasants were being frequently violated and that we were powerless if we didn't organize."

Such transformations are also at the root of the natural growth of new solutions within these movements. The MNFRT cooperatives, for example, pour part of their earnings into solidarity funds that provide financial backing to new cooperatives. Some are formulating projects to educate other workers and involve surrounding communities that supported them through the often fraught and difficult period of taking over the workplace and re-starting production. In Indonesia, the SPI emphasizes solidarity with earthquake and tsunami victims, education and community empowerment, as well as gender equality. The Indian Alliance has made the establishment of savings circles and community-managed micro-finance the bedrock of its organizing and spread both method and solidarity across the Global South by co-founding Shack/Slum Dwellers International. In Brazil, what began as a solution to a straightforward problem has evolved into a movement that fights for agrarian reform for all rural workers and the eventual transformation of society. And in every case, these actions, decisions and innovations come from the grassroots.

Through their participation in La Vía Campesina, both the MST and the SPI embrace the wider agenda of defending smallholding peasants from the depredations of global agribusiness and unfair agricultural trade practices. By linking up peasant farmer groups from eighty-seven countries, including Canada, La Vía Campesina has become a bulwark against the juggernaut of factory farming and the very extinction of small, family-run farms around the world. So while some scholars of social movements consider them successful when they achieve their initial goals and thus lose their reason for being, by acknowledging and taking on an ongoing series of connected problems in the lives of the poor, the ones on which I focus remain active.

The achievements of these social movements suggest noteworthy and potentially far-reaching conclusions. One is the importance of independence, of preserving and protecting autonomous bases within communities of the organized poor. The four social movements studied here have all derived strength from their autonomy from precisely those organizations long considered traditional allies of the poor, such as organized labour and progressive political parties. This infers a new way of thinking about the nature of social change and of the politics that purports or seeks to bring about social change. When the dispossessed encounter and embrace forms of organization and struggle that make sense to them, when they don't abandon a movement once they've won what they set out to win but stay to fight for others, there are, aside from inspiration, a number of political lessons to learn.

Likewise, the idea that localized activity can accomplish more for the poor than a change in government at the national level, even to a popular government, is amply demonstrated here. Even with certain basic rights enshrined in law, too many governments simply ignore them while economic elites throw up new or different forms of the same old problems. In the end, poverty and injustice remain, and the only way to deal with them effectively is through sustained grassroots activity by movements of the poor and oppressed.

There are also, of course, crucial lessons here for organizations involved in poverty-alleviation programs. We need to ask why international institutions disburse funding through local governments or their own outside experts rather than organizations of the poor themselves, and why they are the ones to devise programs and provide so-called expertise. While they may collaborate with international development agencies, progressive political parties and organized labour, vast numbers of hugely disadvantaged people are making it clear that sustainable solutions are only possible through partnership with them. By proposing, managing and carrying out projects themselves, they are demanding — not pleading — to be heard.

Yet rather than welcoming the sense of initiative displayed by movements of the disenfranchised in their struggles for justice, governments ignore them at best and persecute them at worst. In all of the examples in this book, the state has made use of its two main weapons, the police and bureaucracy, to stop change and maintain the status quo. As a result, even though their movements are, without exception, based on the concept of non-violence, the gains the poor have made have not come without many deaths — a fact which only serves to underline their courage and tenacity.

And for the disbursers of overseas development aid, the poor by and large remain "target groups," grateful recipients rather than discerning participants. Most aid organizations, certainly official development agencies, are loathe to work with movements that make no bones about their opposition to sitting governments and their reliance on direct-action strategies. It is ironic that while aid organizations also have a problem with the frequent lack of accountability in those same governments' use of their grants and loans, it is combative social movements that attempt to hold their governments to account.

These movements prove that helplessness and poverty do not make an inescapable equation, that hardship can actually be the matrix from which the poor themselves find the strength and determination to build something successful. By organizing and unleashing their strength and their creativity, millions have already transformed themselves from victims into protagonists and millions more will. Against staggering odds, they are building a vital new definition of success: not the accumulation of wealth and power but the defiance of a socially and economically mandated destiny.

The potential impact of these movements also touches on crucial themes that concern the future of our world. The Landless Rural Workers Movement and the Peasant Union of Indonesia may have found effective and most importantly, sustainable, methods to save our ravaged environment by bringing the issue down to daily-life fundamentals. As an estimated 85 percent of the developing world's urban population is being shoehorned into slums of soul-destroying proportions, slum dwellers' movements may be the key to mitigating their hellish conditions or even transforming them into decent sub-communities within large but liveable cities. The National Movement of Factories Recovered by Workers offers a glimpse of what democratic worker self-management looks like, in not one but a network of such places, challenging the logic of profit-based production. While economic growth waxes and wanes, decreasing and then increasing poverty, its cooperatives serve as a beacon for others who now see running their own workplace as an alternative to unemployment and destitution. They all seem to offer evidence of this wonderful quotation from veteran socialist Tony Benn: "All progress comes from underneath. All real achievements are collective."

All of the stories in this book are ultimately indicative of a new way of thinking about the poor and working class. They bring us to a more profound understanding of the importance of human rights and human ingenuity when we talk about the alleviation of poverty. And while no one is able to foresee the future, I will take a leaf from the optimism of the many poor who have shared their stories with me and assert this: in the struggle against poverty, their success is a blueprint for the better world in which so many of us aspire to live someday.

Part 1

Brazil

A People's Garden

E very time Paulo Barros da Silva planted a fruit tree, concealed within the woods covering the huge ranch where he worked, his boss managed to find and destroy it. Paulo talks about this as he takes the path of fine, deep sand toward his house, opening and closing the heavy wood-rail gates that lock in the small herd of humpbacked cattle resting in the shade of some algarroba trees.

"Whenever I planted a garden," he says, waving an arm in the direction of the river, "he'd let his animals loose on it. When I planted squash, when he noticed how I was getting together some food for my kids, there he'd go, breaking the fence, putting the cattle in there. Every year I planted," he affirms, the matter-of-fact tone rising in a timbre of frustration, "every year during these past six years. And every year he let his cattle loose. It was all gone, from one day to the next."

Paulo speaks with the rural slang and rough accent of Brazil's northeast, one that seems to give short shrift to the words themselves, flying over the syllables until a sentence resembles a rushing train of sound. He comes across as a confident man in spite of everything, square-jawed and voluble, a longish fringe of corkscrew curls beneath the red baseball cap he never seems to remove.

His wife Maria shares with him an air of apparent imperturbability, evident in the straight set of her mouth and the unwavering glance of her dark, feline eyes. They've raised seven children together, two of them still living in the small white-stucco estate house, along with two grandchildren.

Like the rest of the men working on Fazenda Juá, and on similar ranches in the *sertão*, or wild lands, of Pernambuco, Paulo receives a place to live and the legal minimum salary to look after the owner's cattle and sheep. Aside from that he has no rights to any aspect of the land itself.

The couple has never met the ranch's owner, but the animosity they feel for his foreman is such that it verges on the superstitious. Once, says Maria, she gave him a few small hens, partly perhaps to assuage his temper, but also because it is in her nature to be generous. "And the very next day," she recounts, fixing that forthright glance on me, "they were all dead."

"What? The chicks?"

No, it was her flock that was dead. When I ask, slightly confused, how or why they had died, she narrows her eyes and answers succinctly, "*Enveja.*" Which translates as envy, or ill will, but what she meant was the evil eye, the evil eye of Nildo.

"So this estate manager is called Nildo," I affirm. "Erenildo Francisco da Silva."

"I never call him that," says Paulo. "I just call him the foreman — or *o bicho,*" — the animal.

Beyond the wood-slat half doors of Paulo's house, beyond the river called the Riacho do Meio, dun-coloured hills rise steeply, covered with the cacti and thorny scrub trees that characterize the semi-arid landscape of the Brazilian *nordeste*. Overhead, the sky is a vast, pure shade of blue, intense with sunlight and dotted with ponderously restless clouds. And through it swarms the cause of Nildo's penultimate contretemps with the enterprising Paulo: honeybees. In eight clandestine bee boxes set up in scattered patches of brush, they produced the fifty litres of honey he sold in Recife a few weeks earlier. This was another misdeed, for even the winged insects that flew over the estate's 5500 hectares were claimed by its owner, and Paulo was threatened with eviction. While Paulo went to court and was told by a local judge that he and his family could stay, by now he was walking a knife-edge between disaster and the dream of a lifetime.

When I ask Paulo what his first thought was when a small group of families from the Landless Rural Workers Movement suddenly set up a precarious camp of wooden posts and black plastic right in front of the estate, he answers without a moment's hesitation: "To go down and join them. It was. From that day on, I stopped being an employee of the *fazenda* and joined the boys, joined the MST." In fact, he asserted, on every estate he had ever worked, he had always wished the MST would show up and claim it for the landless; he had been waiting for such a moment for years. His next thought, he said, was that the manager and the owner were finally getting what they had long deserved.

In January 1984, as I was preparing to travel to Nicaragua to write about a revolution that had toppled one of Latin America's nastiest dictators, a group of peasants, church workers and trade unionists came together for a meeting in the town of Cascavel, Parana, in the south of Brazil. About 100 people in all, they too lived under the shadow of a dictatorship, in this case, a military one.

These generals were friendly to big business, encouraging industrialization through import substitution, repressing trade unions and promoting a series of changes in agriculture that favoured large-scale, mechanized production for export. Thousands of families were soon moved off of the immense estates that had employed them in seasonal work and allowed them small patches of land to farm for their own benefit. Once evicted, their prospects were bleak; even low-paying industrial jobs were hard to find for people who were often illiterate and whose only skills were tilling the earth or reaping crops. As is the case in many developing countries when peasant farming is abandoned, housing implied, at best, some hovel in the rapidly growing shantytowns and slums of cities unable to absorb the massive inflow of unemployed, and at worst, the street. In Brazil, someone in government came up with the idea of shipping landless peasants up to the Amazon. Several thousand families from the fertile, temperate states of southern Brazil were sent north to the state of Rondonia to attempt farming thin tropical soils in the torrid heat, destroy rain forest and fall prey to repeated epidemics of malaria.

However, most peasants stayed, casting about for odd jobs and bits of land to farm, sometimes on indigenous reserves. A few hundred of them organized and decided to invade and claim local estates where ownership of the land was in question. Today, the names of these places — Macali, Encruzilhado Natalino, Fazenda Annoni — are not only areas of working family farms but evocative emblems of the movement's early history, of physical and psychological victories against the policies of the military regime. To win these, peasant families endured violence, repression and dismal living conditions. But at the same time, they were able to draw on the support of trade unionists and leftwing activists, like João Pedro Stedile, on the Catholic Church's Pastoral Land Commission, and the Lutheran church, which had come to southern Brazil with the flood of German immigrants arriving in the nineteenth century. This support, the linking of their struggles to questions of human rights or even to liberation theology interpretations of gospel, helped transform the way people accustomed to respect the law, to work alone and to regard landowners as their natural superiors, thought about their situation.

Those first few victories encouraged others, and so the goal of the Cascavel meeting was to extend this nascent mobilization over the issue of land reform into a national movement with a name and an identity. And while the brave new dawn of Nicaragua's Sandinista government eventually met the harsh daylight of failure and corruption, in Brazil, the Movimento dos Trabalhadores Rurais Sem Terra (MST) persisted and grew.

By the time of the Fazenda Juá occupation in 2006, the MST had become the largest and most significant grassroots social movement in the Western Hemisphere, if not the world. It is not the first such movement in Brazil's recent history, nor the only one occupying the large space between less radical organizations and more radical ones, such as the Movement of Landless for the Liberation of Land, or MLST. Rather, it has become the primary example for the rural poor in many nations of how a massive grassroots social movement centred on the issue of land tenure can succeed, garnering national and international attention in doing so. In transforming the story of Paulo Barros da Silva, and so many others like him, from one of economic injustice to one of overcoming it, the MST and its achievements constitute an inspiring alternative to the many countervailing pictures of grievance and fruitless protest we see around the world today. By the time of writing, more than 300,000 families all over Brazil had won land through their participation and struggle within this movement. Another 90,000 are still organizing to fight for land, living in squatters' camps as they press the Brazilian government to expropriate and distribute land to them as well. Espousing a combination of radically democratic politics, discipline, environmentalism, innovation and entrepreneurship, membership adds up to some million and a half, an already impressive number that continues to expand.

Yet the MST is only one element brought to a front of globally significant proportions, one pitting the poor and marginalized — the collateral damage of modern ways of doing business — against the status quo. As such it speaks to issues beyond the basic acquisition of land. Like many other successful organizations of the poor, it aims to change the way the poor think and the way those in power think about the poor.

The prominence its members place on literacy and education is one example of this, and arose early on, during the first risky land occupations, when they were attacked by police and hired gunmen, and dismissed as delinquents and scroungers by local townspeople and media alike. In the squatter camps, families either had to find ways to educate children themselves or else send them to local schools, where often the attitude of teachers was inimical to what their parents were doing. Along with an inherent respect for the importance of literacy, they had become increasingly aware of the value of knowledge, of being able to articulate in the courts, to government and to the press the rationale underpinning their activism.

By 2010, the MST had set up 2250 primary and middle schools and trained 3900 teachers in the methods of Paulo Freire's popular education. Maintaining partnerships with thirteen public universities throughout Brazil, more than 300 MST members have studied for degrees in a variety of subjects, while 150,000 adults have achieved basic literacy. Dozens of young people have become doctors after attending medical schools in Cuba or Venezuela, and in May 2006, the MST celebrated as the first *sem terra*, Juvelino Strozake, earned a PhD, in law.

Along with two schools teaching organic agriculture and its own university, members of the MST also successfully run scores of small businesses, cooperatives and shops. They organize regional and national conferences, provide courses, run campaigns and publish a newspaper and a magazine every month. Yet if the government were to do its job properly, the MST might not even exist.

For a large nation with a dynamic economy based on oil, manufacturing and commodity exports, ownership of land is still heavily weighted towards a small group of people, a very small group: less than 1 percent of the population owns 43 percent of the land in Brazil. Mostly they do just that — own it; they hire others to wrangle their cattle or plant sugar cane, soya beans or eucalyptus, in some cases, leaving it fallow for decades as they wait for its fiscal value to slowly increase. For many wealthy businessmen, like Fazenda Juá's proprietor, Slaibe Hatem, ownership of one or several *fazendas* remains an important symbol of personal status. Hatem, for example, lived a couple hundred miles away from his vast landholding, in Recife, from where he ran a chain of department stores called Lojas Maraja. Were even half of Fazenda Juá's 5500 hectares of wilderness to be expropriated and divided up into fifteen hectare lots, 150 poor families would be able to produce food and earn a living there, rather than one man raising a few dozen head of sheep and cattle, essentially as a hobby.

Over the years, several Brazilian presidents have promised to carry out land reform — expressing a recognition of the problem as much as an attempt to win votes — but they have inevitably fallen well short of their commitments. Agrarian reform is even enshrined in the nation's constitution, which allows for lands either belonging to the state or deemed unproductive to be divided up and given to rural families. There is also a government institute for agrarian reform, the INCRA, whose mandate is to carry out the evaluations of such areas and provide credits to buy basic farm equipment and seeds. The government pays landowners for their acreages, although often they are expropriated in lieu of unpaid taxes.

Nonetheless, in 2006, there were an estimated 12 million landless peasants in Brazil and 23 million rural workers living below the poverty line. As Rubinilsa Leandro de Souza, MST co-coordinator for education in Pernambuco, explained it, going ahead and occupying large unproductive estates is "the only way. There is no agrarian reform in this country. What there is," she said, "is a compensatory policy of resolving social conflicts." In other words, the MST, in some ways, brings about the "conflict," or the social pressure, so that the state will finally fulfil what the nation's constitution already stipulates.

In trying to account for why the MST has thrived where so many others have withered away, there are several places to search for clues. Among the participants at Cascavel was Dom Pedro Casaldáliga, bishop of São Felix do Araguaia, well-known for his championing of the rights of peasant farmers in a region of the Amazon with a reputation for violence and lethal conflicts over land. According to Jan Rocha and Sue Branford's definitive history of the MST, *Cutting the Wire*, it was he who suggested that, "If the movement learns to walk on its own feet, it will go much further." He was voicing what a number of families had already figured out: this notion of autonomy — independence from the church, non-governmental organizations and unions, and from politics with a view to governance, as opposed to political activism — is key to the movement's strength. What's more, this independence revolves around the idea that a community with a problem can manage its own solution, rather than leaving it in the hands of a particular power group or leadership, a belief replicated in other grassroots social movements in other nations struggling around different issues.

"Taken together, the decisions reached at this meeting show that, even at this early stage, the *sem terra* were consciously attempting to create an organization that was different from anything that had previously existed in Brazil," wrote Rocha and Branford. Its members "saw themselves as a new type of exploited worker — people who had been expelled from the land by agricultural modernization — and as such, they needed their own movement that could respond in an appropriate fashion. They believed that their struggle for land was part of a broader revolutionary movement to end exploitation and to create a more just society for everyone. Their vision was unashamedly utopian, and in that lay much of its appeal to the poor and excluded."

Another key feature of the MST's success came out of a decision taken by the membership at another, much larger congress, held the following year in Curitiba. In seeking to devise a structure that would avoid the possibility of a small clique of leaders ever dominating the movement, they set up elected collective bodies instead, each in charge of specific functions, such as recruitment, training or financial matters.

Horácio Martins de Carvalho, a Brazilian agronomist and consultant, described this structure in his study of the MST, in *Another Production Is Possible*: "To take charge of local, regional, state and national struggles, there are ten active sectoral collectives," he wrote, "at the national level and at the level of each of the 23 federal states and of the federal district in which the MST is an effective presence. In addition to this, there are on average four to seven regional directorates within each federal state. Each level of decision-making, from the settlement to the various regional, state and national directorates has relative autonomy. The dynamics of study, reflection and debate over the themes of the national meetings and congresses can be used as an illustration: the themes are debated at all levels, from the grassroots units — composed of neighbouring families within a settlement — up to the national directorate."

From its earliest days, therefore, it was agreed that policies would be dictated by people engaged in struggles, in the regions, with decisions flowing upwards from below. One national policy that was discarded, for example, mandated collective farming on the resettled land. People didn't like it; the process didn't work very well, and in 1994, after much discussion and evaluation, it was changed for one whereby each settlement decided for itself how it would manage production. Organic farming and the establishment of cooperatives, while heavily promoted, are other matters members themselves have to decide. While not perfect, internal democracy is recognized as essential, even logical, to the functioning of the MST. "The leadership listens to what the grassroots has to say," said Itelvina Mazioli, an MST leader. "We get things wrong and we change policy after protests from the base."

For Carvalho, "the hundreds of decision-making centres related to the mass character of the MST give this movement its own dynamics: the diversity and velocity of the changes in the co-relation of political and ideological forces do not lend themselves to the hardening of bureaucratic organizational structures, either within the directorates or the sectoral collectives. One of the reasons for this lies in the origins of the MST: the occupation of land."

Pointing out how hundreds, even thousands of families, are often mobilized to occupy land, Carvalho added, "It would be extremely difficult to imagine, however great the discipline in such mass actions might be, that the organization of such an event could be managed by a bureaucratically hardened structure."

Clearly an important factor in the movement's success, such participatory democracy is a feature we shall see in other movements of the poor, situated in other, very different geographical and cultural spaces.

In 1985, as Brazil's military government gave way to a civilian presidency elected by a college of deputies, 50,000 families were taking part in dozens of small occupations, mostly in the southern states. In October of that year, the movement headed north, with the first occupation in the state of Espiritu Santo. It continued to spread throughout the 1980s, to Alagoas, Minas Gerais, Sergipe and Ceara. By the end of the decade, its tally was more than 80,000 families, living in 730 settlements covering 3.6 million hectares of farmland.

Meanwhile large landowners had begun to organize themselves in response, using both armed security and their connections to the nation's lawmakers to try to hold on to their property. By the time president Jose Sarney finished his term in 1989, he had settled 84,852 families, most of them in the Amazon. He had promised land to 1.4 million families. So as the movement entered more and more regions of the country, its members had learned that they could expect nothing from politicians; they would have to conquer land through mobilization and occupation, by applying pressure on INCRA and on the state in general, through blockades and protest marches.

Subsequent administrations proved to be increasingly hostile towards the MST, invading its offices and tapping phones, one of the most egregious governments being that of Fernando Henrique Cardoso, president from 1995 to 2003. In January 2001, Cardoso announced with great aplomb that, over the previous five years, he had carried out the "largest land reform program in the world," peacefully settling 482,000 families on plots of land. Yet behind this statement, the reality was quite different. "To arrive at these numbers," wrote Manuel Domingos, a professor at the University of Ceara, "the government not only had to count old land redistributions as new ones, but reinvent a common practice from the time of the military dictatorship: counting formal recognition of land title as redistribution."

In fact, Cardoso's economic policies had made small-scale farming so unviable that rural poverty had actually grown to envelope almost 60 percent of the total population, up from 39.2 percent. More than four million families abandoned rural areas between 1995 and 1999. And in 1996, in the state of Para, military police attacked a protest march of MST members, killing nineteen of them, a massacre that lives on in MST lore and its famous *misticas*, the political theatricals that adorn everything from educational events to regional and national conferences.

Cardoso also passed a new law, striking at one of the movement's central strategies. This law stipulated a two-year delay for any occupied estate before INCRA would even begin to undertake the study to decide whether or not that land was unproductive. In other words, he imposed a mandatory two years of camp life, two years where absolutely nothing would be done, while landless families tried to survive as best they could on hope and handouts. But just as the movement had learned to retreat in the face of attacks by police or hired guns, only to re-occupy the next day, they also began to occupy the margins around an estate rather than the property itself. Some landowners responded by actually building fake camps on their land to assure themselves of that two-year respite. Little wonder then, that in spite of his inability to carry out the massive agrarian reform he too had always promised, the previous president, Luiz Inácio da Silva of the Workers Party, had at least, said Rubinilsa, "given us breathing space."

It was Paulo who told the twenty or so families living on the grassy verge by the side of the road that, in fact, an INCRA employee had visited the estate several years back. In this case, the two-year waiting period would not apply; Fazenda Juá had already been deemed unproductive. So in early May, they walked through the gate and up the drive with their children and their few possessions to set up a new camp under the roofs of a pair of cavernous, open-sided storage sheds.

The shade of the roofs and the towering trees nearby, the proximity of tapped water and even a cement-walled bathhouse represented a marked improvement in living standards. Yet there was no avoiding an initial impression of deprivation and squalor: open fires on the cement flooring, blackened pots of day-old rice and beans, the paltry, tattered belongings the poor hold on to no matter how worn-out, flies everywhere. Water came from a tap over a cement cattle trough and was only turned on for a couple hours a day, after a fight with Nildo, who cut off the supply completely for a few days until the men threatened to shut off his water by severing the main pipe. The toilets were only flushed out with pails of water once a day or so, and taking a shower meant a trip to the stalls with a bucket and empty cooking-oil tin.

A man named José Paulo lived with his wife and tiny daughter in a truck back of brightly painted slats, its door a piece of old tarp advertising Skol beer. A family of five, Alexandre, Lucia and their three children, had set up in a pen of corrugated roofing against one wall, while at the opposite end of the shed, behind a tall stack of raw lumber, lived the taciturn Santos brothers, their wives and between them a total of seven children, all but two under five years of age. Cleonesio da Silva, who everyone called Lula, slept in a makeshift tent he'd erected by flinging a blue plastic tarp over a beam.

Two more families occupied the old hay barn, and this is where I would also live for the length of my stay there, along with Damião Oliveira, barely past his teens and in charge of training, or *formação*. Next door to us were Manoel Correia, his wife Cissa and their little girl Rosilene. At thirty-three, Manoel had been without great prospects most of his life, ever since his father had been expelled from an estate because the owner considered him too old to work for him anymore. However, Manoel was well-spoken and educated compared to most of the other camp dwellers, for he had worked with a Catholic foundation for the poor in the nearby city of Arco Verde; he had learned carpentry as well but never found a job and preferred farming just the same. "No, there's no way you can save money to buy a piece of land," he explained. "The salaries are very low here in Brazil. So that's why I'm here, to win a piece of land and earn our daily bread."

While the living conditions of the men hired to look after the cattle were, in fact, little better than those of the camp dwellers, a short distance away, as if on another planet, Nildo lived in a suburban-style house with a satellite dish, telephone wires and a late-model car parked in the car port. Behind his home was the estate office, long closed, the row of trophies in the window garnered by Slaibe Hatem's prize-winning Nelore cattle gathering dust. Behind this, and surrounded by wire fencing, was Hatem's neat, pink-stucco house, solidly shut, a swing hanging from the branch of one of the tallest algarroba trees.

The hay barn had been divided into two, and the part where I stayed had become the home of a deaf man named Celestino and his sister Moça. Its scarred brick walls were pocked with wasp nests, and its lofty rafters the redoubt of a pair of bats that flew and swooped so swiftly it was impossible to even distinguish their colour, just the endless circular motions they made all night long. From the earthen floor in a corner near the battered door, the smoke of an open fire rose past a line strung with gutted fish folded like ancient leather wallets, up and out the narrow opening between the tile roof and brick wall. Pretty much everything was done on, and stored on, the ground: it was where food was prepared and dishes washed, where the family's most basic possessions — scabby plastic bowls and cups, a jar of cheap, bent flatware, the thermos, boxes of dusty clothing — were arranged along two walls. Inside the modest screen of a hanging sheet, at the foot of the hard wooden pallet that served as Moça's bed, sat a rusty metal machine for grinding forage.

Accompanying the discomfort were concerns over food. INCRA was on strike that summer in Pernambuco, which meant the basic government food rations of rice, beans, cornmeal and oil distributed via charities and social organizations had been held up for months. Most of what was there had been donated by Paulo, who used the proceeds from selling his honey to buy rice and beans for every family. Aside from this, the men strung out fishing nets in the river, gathered honey and sold charcoal made from fallen trees.

That life here was harsh and uncompromising was a fact etched on the faces of the first few people I met, of Alexandra from the truck back with her slumped shoulders, and Lucia, with her lumpy body and air of permanent weariness, who found the idea of my staying there simply unfathomable. At times it seemed almost as if they had all been led astray somehow into this dramatic impasse, had stumbled into something they could barely describe beyond a few short sentences. Yet in an odd kind of aesthetic contrast to this hardscrabble inurement to misery were the birds. Almost every family had a few — red-cowled cardinals with their scarlet caps, ultramarine grosbeaks, ruddy ground doves, seedeaters and seed-finches — in homemade cages hung from grimy walls and old pieces of farm machinery, feathers brilliant in the sunlight. Like substitutes, it struck me, for pictures on a wall, or for a television set, not so much adornments as reflections captured from the mirror of the land they hoped some day would be theirs.

Life for the peasant farmer of Pernambuco, and the northeast in general, had always been tough, the parched landscape and persistent class divisions long the background of novels and film, and of Brazil's popular television soap operas. "I'm used to working," said seventy-eight-year-old Cicero Lyra da Silva, explaining his reason for still seeking land to farm at his age. "That's what my life is all about, work."

Things got tougher and less folkloric in the 1970s, when the Brazilian government responded to that decade's global oil crisis with a plan to use fuel made from sugar cane alcohol. In a kind of reverse agrarian reform, powerful business interests, avid for the subsidies being offered as part of the Pro-Alcool Program, moved quickly and ruthlessly to expand their holdings. Between 1975 and 1989, an estimated $10.5 billion of taxpayer money went to big cane growers, as thousands of smallholding peasants were evicted, their gardens and pastures replaced by vast extensions of sugar. It should have been fertile ground for the MST, yet it took over three years to organize the first occupation in Pernambuco, in 1989. And while only 14,000 families had been resettled there by 2006, it had become one of the movement's fastest growing sectors.

This fact was apparent at the conference of educational workers at the Paulo Freire Centre, built on a former estate near the city of Caruaru, where hundreds of young people had come together for three days of meetings. They filled the cafeteria at meal times, slept cheek by jowl in dormitories and assembled for lectures and *misticas* in the main hall, its doorway guarded by two cement busts I first thought were biblical characters, perhaps put there by the former owners, but which turned out to be Paulo Freire, with his long beard, and Che Guevara, his beret looking more like a turban.

At the conference I met a man named Roberto Bras, who was giving a course to troubled youth from Caruaru. Roberto had joined the MST the previous year, he told me, after half a lifetime of working as a letter carrier in São Paulo, far from the bright and open skies of the northeast, growing accustomed to its cold, rainy winters but never its depressing urban poverty. The kind of person who spent his savings to accumulate a set of encyclopaedias, volume by volume, he was an autodidact, an amateur student of nature, full of plans for the day when he would, he hoped, receive a piece of land on an estate called Papagaio, a few miles north, near São Caetano da Raposa. Roberto had already calculated its potential: the nutritional value of the algarroba, the arid yet fertile soil, the miraculous aid of nitrogen-fixing plants, even the waste products of the camp itself — animal manure, ashes and phosphorous from ground-up rocks. "It's close to the highway," he said of Papagaio, "so we can start growing organic vegetables and fruit, and sell them to passers-by on the road."

But in explaining why he had joined the MST, that enthusiasm drained for a moment, and he became emotional, almost tearful. He joined because he considered his life a failure: "I've always worked, and worked hard; I've never stolen, I've never cheated, I've never done anything dishonest," he said, counting these attributes off on the fingers of one hand. "I've never done anything that would impinge upon my personal integrity. And what do I have to show for it at the age of forty? Nothing." He had simply reached the point one day, he concluded, where he either resigned himself to a life of poverty or did something to change everything.

While Roberto just happened to be particularly loquacious compared to the average Pernambucano perhaps, the story of every person who decided to join the MST and go through the arduous business of claiming land was as evocative as his of the realities of poverty, of its accompanying sense of failure, of humiliation, in trying to do what is right over an entire lifetime, yet never achieving what you'd always hoped you would. The people of Fazenda Juá personified the human raw material of which a viable demo-cratic movement is eventually formed. Attracted to the movement by the handbills its frontline workers, or *frente de massa*, routinely hand out in poor neighbourhoods all over the country, they didn't necessarily arrive with no-tions of social justice or specialized knowledge or even a way of articulating their situation; they brought nothing but their needs, for the most part, their individual crises — and this is where someone like Bethania came in.

Bethania Cardoso was the new regional coordinator in Arco Verde, one of thirteen in the state of Pernambuco. While, like Damião, she looked like a teenager at first glance, she was only a year shy of thirty and the mother of three little girls. When she herself was a child, her mother had won land in Escadas, in what is called the Zona da Mata, or Forest Zone, near the state's tropical coast. But she hadn't been all that interested in the MST while growing up, Bethania said, working at various jobs over the years, as a cleaner, a shop assistant, sometimes a teacher. "Suddenly, about five years ago, I became interested in camping myself," she told me. "I was in a camp for a year, where I became the teacher. Eventually I worked in all of the different sectors in the camp, and after that, I was invited to join the regional coordination, in charge of the sector for gender, where I spent a year. Then I was in charge of a micro-region for less than a year, then of the whole region itself, in the Zona da Mata Sul." Only a few weeks earlier, she had been asked to move to Arco Verde and assume the regional coordination there.

It was Bethania's job to work with nine different settlements and camps in the region, Fazenda Jardim Jatoba, which had gone through a gruelling eight-year occupation being the toughest, Fazenda Juá, the newest. She did so with a very small staff and few resources, taking public transport the half-hour ride out to the camp as often as she could. Upon arrival, she would gather everyone into a circle, warming up these general meetings with a few standard MST slogans. "Eme-ese-te," she shouted, raising a fist. "Occupy! Resist! Produce!" everyone shouted back in reply. There were more such slogans, as well as a song or two, and then everyone got down to business. There was still no end in sight to the INCRA strike; various courses were being offered and anyone interested was invited to sign up; this week, the medicinal plants and collective vegetable gardens would be planted.

The *acampados* had elected Paulo as their representative, and divided into three nuclei of ten people, each with two more reps, a man and a woman. Then came the different sectors: Paulo also headed the sector on production, Maria the sector for health, because of her knowledge of medicinal plants, Manoel, who would begin adult literacy classes the following week, for education, and Lucia, for gender.

These duties not only gave people tasks to fulfil but also stimulated a continual communication among them. They represented the first steps toward some kind of organization, to dealing with problems rather than just complaining about them and to taking responsibility for how the camp was run. Bethania might make suggestions on nocturnal security, or on not leaving garbage lying around, but every decision had to be voted on. Problems with alcohol, slacking off, mistreating a spouse — all of these might crop up in any poor community, but every issue would have to be dealt with by the camp members themselves.

Communal work periods would also begin that week, Bethania announced, twice a week, from seven in the morning until ten, with one group clearing land for the vegetable garden, the other cleaning up the camp site. "People who don't understand us just love to say that the poor are dirty, but we know that's not true," she declared. "There's no reason for everyone's place not to be swept and tidy. You should see the camp at Our Lady of Carmel, not even a piece of scrap paper on the ground."

"What about if I get some paying work for a day and can't make it?" asked one man.

"Work it out with your reps," she said, "and they can give you something else, an extra night of patrolling, maybe, to do."

That both of these projects would bring obvious and much needed improvements to camp life was apparent the morning of the first communal work period, the next day. One group, including Celestino and Manoel's wife Cissa, swept through the camp with brooms and pails of water. The collected garbage was put into a barrow and hauled off, the bath house scrubbed out, ashes carted away, even the ground between the barn and storage sheds raked clean of twigs and pebbles.

Another group went down to the plot of land picked out near the river after the meeting, where they chopped away at the grass and caster plants with scythes and machetes. Once the vegetation had dried, they would burn it and hoe it underground. Free seedlings were coming from the mayor's office in Arco Verde and from Jardim Jatoba. Initially they would plant fast-growing vegetables, such as beans and squash, which would be ready to eat in a few weeks, then potatoes, melon, manioc and corn.

These structures would remain throughout the life of the group as a squatters' camp and on into its existence as a settlement, what the MST calls "agro-villas" of small landholding peasants. They were often, although not always, the basis for cooperative enterprises that helped keep these farming communities on their feet.

Bethania called this structuring and collective work "organicity," and credited it with the success of the MST. "Other movements," she said, "don't succeed in organizing themselves in this way; they don't understand why we grow every day or why we win so much land. It's the way we organize ourselves, the way we apply pressure on the authorities, the way we give hope to people and transform them into a new man or a new woman."

The transformation of all of those people I met, with all of their doubts, fears and prejudices, was as much the point of the MST as the simple acquisition of land. "It takes a lot of explaining, a lot of lectures," said Bethania. "People come to the camp often with a different vision than our vision; they don't understand the process of struggle. So we bring together the sectors, we talk about politics, give lectures on the movement, so that they really understand what the movement is all about. Some people come just because they want some land, or just because of the food rations, because they don't have anything to eat, they don't have jobs."

The process of transformation doesn't happen overnight or even from one month to the next, she emphasized, "because you have to take someone who doesn't have any knowledge at all, and think you are going to clear that up all at once? No. It's a slow process. Sometimes it's easy to change the way a person thinks; they have that curiosity, that open mind. With others it is difficult. It's 'I just want some land,' and that's it."

The need to change the way people with problems think about themselves, about their place in society and about the problem itself, explains the prominence placed on education and *formação* — best described perhaps as the study of political history and ideas that challenge accepted notions of what is correct and fair and what is not; intellectual weapons, in a sense, to defend their actions.

And while these come from an assortment of sometimes conflicting political ideas, this doesn't seem to matter. Examples of guerrilla action divorced from the rest of society, or revolutionary objectives dispensed from above, are just as laudable as working-class action. Rather than working out the implications of every political concept, any one of them or any historical figure that seems supportive of the struggle of the poor and landless have their own inspirational value.

Che Guevara, for example, is seen not as a person whose political beliefs would never have brooked the kind of participatory democracy prevalent in the settlements and camps, but a martyred symbol of the fight against capitalist exploitation and selfish individualism. Cuba is not seen as a country where the working class is extraordinarily underpaid and unable to independently organize itself, but one where education and health are free, where United States hegemony is challenged daily. It is as if there is a continual search for examples of the heroic, and that can be Che or Chico

Mendes, eighteenth-century runaway slave Zumbi das Palmares or Sister Dorothy Stang, murdered by ranchers in Amapa in 2005. In some ways these examples are moral rather than political, opening up interpretations of the political by a focus on the parts that are admirable or useful rather than the intellectual consequences. In fact, the consequences are visible in the result of being in the MST in the way its members lead their lives.

From the beginning, however, the dominant ideology of the MST, was simply one that challenged capitalism and the way it not only creates masses of poor but relegates them to crime-ridden *favelas* in the cities and sordid huts in the countryside. MST members talk about and advocate socialism yet, interestingly, without a very defined picture of — or internecine arguments about — what exactly they mean by this. "A society without exploiters or exploited," was how it was put back in 1985 at the Curitiba congress, a series of ideas about what a fair and just society ought to be like, where members should discuss and come to free-standing decisions, where solidarity and altruism are virtues.

And while some see a contradiction between the essentially conservative ideas of country people with their emphasis on the importance of owning land, traditional family structures and religious faith, it is perhaps a mistake to see this as anything but logical. Like the workers who run their own factories in Argentina, studied in Part Four, the vast majority of MST members must concentrate on production in order to sustain themselves and their families. At the same time, the existence of a more militant layering within the movement that posits and promotes certain ideals and aspirations of a more just world can provide a healthy alternative to traditional ways of seeing Brazilian society with all its contradictions. Some MST members may agree or identify with such ideals, while others may remain unmoved by them yet welcome in the movement as a whole. So while the discourse may be radical, the daily routine is highly pragmatic: how to get land, how to make that land flourish, how to set up a school, get good prices for produce and so on.

What's more, while the organization handles large amounts of money, no one has become rich and no one profits from their post, unlike many Workers Party leaders and their cronies. Voluntarism is not only encouraged but also very popular, particularly among the children and grandchildren of settlers. They earn no more than minimum salary and a place to live for their often-long hours. As thirty-year-old Jose Batista de Oliveira, a member of the national coordination representing the state of São Paulo, put it, "You don't do the job for money but because of your understanding, your convictions."

The development of young, organic leaders has been attributed by many students of the movement to its success. "It is through the work of these leaders that direct action remains a primary movement strategy because, although the movement is strategically scaling up, (they) continue to work locally in the struggle for land, mobilizing people for occupations, organizing in the settlements, and recruiting and training new leaders who then move to new places to carry out these same activities," wrote Brenda Baletti, Tamara Johnson and Wendy Wolford. This work is highlighted in every copy of the *Jornal Sem Terra*, in interviews each month with a different home-grown activist, whose stories of participation in occupations, of strong, even emotional, engagement with the struggle and rise to leadership positions through formal training and organizing work are remarkably similar.

In fact, political *formação* could be problematic if it did not take place within the context of the emphasis on education in general, "a fundamental element for the construction of men and women to freely decide their own destiny," as one member put it. Both are related to the movement's need to continually develop new cadres and local leaders but also to the provision of intellectual tools to every member. At Fazenda Juá, for example, some of the older children were able to take a free bus to the primary school in nearby Moderna, while others had been left with relatives in nearby towns to continue attending classes. In the case of Alexandre and Lucia's children, however, the family had moved so many times, they were by now several years behind their peers. The elder daughter, Vanessa, fourteen, was only in the equivalent of about grade four or five, something about which she couldn't help but feel ashamed.

From the early days of the MST's existence, the children of the camps, the *sem terrinhas*, as they are called, have been through Vanessa's dilemma. In spite of their early years, many of them actively participate in camp life, gaining a broader understanding of social and political contexts than the vast majority of children their age. For them and their parents, the struggle for land not only prefigured the importance of education but a particular kind of education, one that fits in with the cultural and personal revolutions they have lived.

Yet it has been mostly the lack of decent schools for the rural poor that created a void that had to be filled with something different. And into that void, they have put the teaching method developed by Paulo Freire: popular education. For Rubinilsa de Souza, it was as much the basis of the movement's democracy as the training of cadre, as much at the heart of its success as the attaining of land. "Popular education," she said, "is what gives a sense of protagonism to the subject."

The author of *Pedagogy of the Oppressed*, and one of the greatest educational thinkers of the twentieth century, Freire originally developed his method in the 1950s, proving that he could teach illiterate adults to read in forty-five days by situating educational activity in the lived experience of its participants and developing their consciousness. Referring to a standard teaching phrase for children as an example, he wrote, "It is not enough to teach 'Eva viu a uva' (Eva saw the grape), if we don't know Eva's position in the social context, who produced the grape, and who profited from its production."

Rubinilsa also pointed out how liberation theology, the religious philosophy underpinning the zeal of those Catholic lay workers and clergy who first helped in the formation of the MST, had also brought consciousness raising to its work among the poor. "That is what gives our movement this characteristic," she added, "that of the peasants themselves in the process of struggle. Since these two currents give a voice and autonomy, empower the workers, by necessity you have to have a structure that backs this up. It can't just be your discourse; if you have a certain concept of an organization, the organization has to respond to that concept."

Thus, even before the first seeds were planted in their communal garden, the families of Fazenda Juá were already thinking about a school. They had chosen, for this purpose, an empty cement shed just beyond the ranch workers' dismal cottages. There, the camp's illiterate adults and growing contingent of children would learn by using texts and materials developed by the MST, a curriculum that by then was being offered to more than 200,000 children and adolescents. With it, they were learning not only how to read and write, but just as importantly perhaps, to assess reality. Rather than show up how few grades she has passed, Vanessa's education in an MST-run school would help her understand how much she has achieved, in a world that has given her few chances.

Those chances grew even dimmer when the MST families were violently expelled by local police from Fazenda Juá, shortly after my visit. During this period, the police often drove by to see Nildo, "dropping in for their *cafezinho*," Lula would say. Within the month, Nildo succeeded in charging Paulo Barros da Silva and several others with the possession of dangerous weapons — in this case, hunting rifles. Bethania managed to have them released after one night, and everyone moved to Our Lady of Carmel, including Paulo and Maria, who had now lost their house. With still no food packages from INCRA, a number of families had no choice but abandon the occupation. In desperation, those remaining decided to re-occupy the estate, which meant that Paulo had violated his release conditions. Once again, he was jailed, this time for two weeks. By the end of the year, the families had regrouped along the margins of the road running past Fazenda Juá, frequently harassed by gunmen, apparently hired by Slaibe Hatem and based on the estate, driving around the camp in jeeps shooting off their rifles.

By then, the caged birds had been set free, the communal garden in its sea of grass and thorny shrub left to wither and the hopes for a quick expropriation dashed. It was not, however, the end of the story of Fazenda Juá.

A People's Production

Just as Fazenda Juá afforded a glimpse of how the struggle for land can begin, the settlement of Bom Pastor — the Good Shepherd — presented one of what can happen once that struggle has been won.

Bom Pastor was situated near a small, tidy city called Teodoro Sampaio, in the south of São Paulo state, on the border of Parana. Heading out of the city, the bank of the Parana River was visible in the distance, and much closer up, two straggling lines of black tarp shacks along one side of the two-lane highway. Even in an area with two decades of activity, there were still lands to claim here — ranches and sugar plantations — for the rural workers of what is known as the Pontal de Paranapanema.

A few miles down a gravel road lay the farm of Antonio Camargo, its simple one-storey house surrounded by trees, outbuildings and extensive gardens. I had heard about Antonio from the middle of his three sons, Roberval, an agronomist at the MST's new agro-ecology school near Itapeva, but we didn't spend a lot of time on chitchat. Rather, it was almost as if Antonio felt he had to give me a sort of crash course on the MST.

A tall lanky man, he spoke in a pontificating style intended, I felt, to mask a certain shyness, about the lack of justice in Brazilian society. "When you see the mother of a family mix a little sugar with water to feed her children, to fill their bellies so they can sleep that night, a human being begins to feel a sense of revolt from within," he said, to a soundtrack of squabbling chickens outside. "Or a man go door to door, looking for a job. They have to go to the land. They have to. And that is what has happened here."

Another bugbear was the media, one source, he believed, of the discrimination even settlers still felt when they went to the city to sell their produce. "The media doesn't come out here," he asserted with his singsong delivery, "they don't show what I have here. They don't show the freezer full of meat to eat; they don't show the thirty sheep I have in the meadow, the fish in the fishpond, the shed I have for the silk worms. They don't show how we live; they don't show any of that. So people don't know anything about us. They're afraid of us."

Ninety-two families lived in Bom Pastor, all of them with prosperous farms of 14 hectares each, brick houses with running water and modern electrical appliances, cars or trucks parked in their driveways — a world away from the lives of the people in Fazenda Juá in Pernambuco — and from their origins.

Antonio's farm was a model of what financial planners advise: diversification. Along with planting the many stands of trees — mostly eucalyptus but also palm, fruit and olive — he had dug a pond and filled it with tilapia, built twelve bee boxes, and fenced pasture for his cows and sheep. He and twenty other families had also begun raising silk worms, purchasing the eggs from a local textile company, then proceeding to feed them the tons of mulberry leaves they consumed daily from the three hectares of bushes he planted on former grasslands, before selling back the cocoons for a modest profit.

The gardens around his house produced a grocer's variety of produce, from vegetables and fruit to coffee and cinnamon, contributing to his family's self-sufficiency and careful use of income. Antonio had a system whereby he moved his cattle into wooded areas during the dry season, leaving pieces of pasture fallow, as well as an ingenious method of mixing their salt blocks with the ground-up leaves of various medicinal plants to keep them healthy without drugs or hormones.

It was, however, his tree nursery next to the driveway that kept him and his family busiest. Breakfast over, Antonio went to the fridge and began pulling out dozens of plastic bags filled with seeds, all neatly labelled. "A lot of people are completely unacquainted with them," he said proudly, as he brought the lot to the dining table. "They don't even know that they still exist, what I've kept here." For years, Antonio had been collecting the seeds of native trees and plants that had all but disappeared from the Pontal region.

Antonio Camargo's life began fifty-two years earlier in circumstances that couldn't be further from his current situation. Born in the north of the state of Espiritu Santo, near Bahia, his family was so large and so poor that he left them while still a child, to work in a textile plant at the age of fourteen. When still a young man and in spite of the military dictatorship, he became involved in agitating for union rights; nothing all that revolutionary — "At the time men came to work barefoot," he said. "We simply demanded uniforms and boots."

Nonetheless, this activity brought him to the attention of the police, and he decided to flee to the Araguaia region in the southern Amazon and join the small guerrilla movement then operating there. He didn't last long: shortly after he arrived, he said, the leader of his band was killed in an army ambush. The boys in the rear guard escaped, and Antonio began a life on the run, working on ranches all over the country. Eventually, he married and settled on the banks of the Parana River but was soon moved from there, along with hundreds of other families, to make way for a hydroelectric project. Some of the displaced, including Antonio, got construction jobs on the dam site or in the electricity plant. But when it was privatized by the Cardoso government in 1993, Antonio was laid off — "left on the side of the road," as he put it. As his son Roberval remembers it, "We had two choices, join the MST or go live in a *favela* in Teodoro Sampaio." Antonio decided to join the MST.

The Pontal was, in fact, a region well known for its highly irregular land status. Heavily forested until the 1940s, large pieces of it were essentially stolen by people who faked land titles and then cleared them for cattle and sugar cane. Their procedures could be as brutal as they were thorough: on one day in 1973, an entire 5000-hectare swathe of forest was sprayed with defoliants containing Agent Orange, destroying the trees and killing hundreds of animals, including tapir and jaguars. The MST, which arrived there in the early 1990s, considered the region ideal for its expansion. Not only was it close enough to São Paulo to grab plenty of media attention, it was well known that much of the land there had been illegally occupied.

Jose Rainha, a boyhood friend of Antonio's from Espiritu Santo and MST organizer, was travelling throughout the region at the time, inviting rural workers and displaced peasants to meetings. "He told us there was land available for us," Antonio said, "state lands or unproductive lands. So we joined, and along with 2780 families went to the Primeiro do Abril camp in 1994." When Primeiro do Abril was expropriated a year later, however, there was not enough land for so many families. "We, all of us, made the decision about who would stay," he went on, "the neediest families, or the ones with the most children." Antonio, his wife, Marta, and their sons moved on to a second camp nearby.

"Our first three days there, it was nothing but lead pouring down on us," he recalled. "The black tarp was blown full of holes and we had to lie flat on the ground the whole time; we couldn't move, couldn't eat. One fellow was shot in the leg; a pregnant woman was also hit. Three days like that we were."

This ranch was also expropriated, but once again, there was not enough land for all the families. The Camargo family moved for the third time, but as if in divine recompense, its owner decided from the beginning that he would negotiate the expropriation of his property. Ninety-two families were given lots, and Antonio set about transforming ground that was so degraded by ranching that parts of it were desert.

Eight years later, this was difficult to even picture; tall trees shaded the roads and grew in large clumps throughout the landscape. Houses surrounded by fruit trees and flowers dotted the area, next to green fields of crops and grassy pastures dotted with milk cows and sheep. Life had been coaxed back into one of the most environmentally devastated areas the MST had ever conquered, and because they were not using chemicals in their fields and gardens, farmers were earning top prices for organic produce.

Yet at first the settlers who had won land after so much hardship thought only about replicating the farming methods of the large landowners they had fought against — often the only methods they knew. They too wanted the most modern hybrid seeds, to use lime and chemical fertilizers for the highest crop yields possible and, to get rid of pests quickly and easily, *jogando veneno*, as farmers themselves so phlegmatically put it — literally, throwing poison. And as a result, they became caught up in the vicious cycle of unsustainable agriculture, needing to buy more and more herbicide, more and more fertilizer and incurring ever-larger debts to maintain production.

This new problem — and its organic solution — has been and continues to be discussed and dissected by the MST. An example of a policy brought up from below, many individual farmers and settlements had begun trying organic farming years before it became an issue for the organization as a whole. As reports of their success spread slowly throughout the movement and greater numbers of its members saw the advantages of sustainable methods, the emphasis on organic eventually assumed proportions similar to that placed on popular education.

In the Pontal region, the Ecological Research Institute, or IPE, was around the same time looking for ways to save the almost extinct black lion tamarin living in a remnant of Atlantic rain forest on a mountain called the Morro do Diabo. They began to work with a small number of settlers, offering them free seedlings and encouraging them to plant woodlots linking the Morro with other fragments of forest where the little monkey might expand its habitat. By 1999, these families had planted 100,000 trees, and their enthusiasm convinced IPE to think about helping them revive their lots of land as well. There were plenty of useful species — fruit trees, cashew and leucaena — that could be grown alongside crops, improving yields as well as soil quality, and certain benign varieties of eucalyptus, such as *camaldulensis*, good for soil and stopping erosion. These were the kind planted throughout Bom Pastor.

Starting with a few seedlings from IPE, Antonio set up the nursery, which, by 2005, was selling 90,000 seedlings every month. The IPE was now buying from him, as were a number of local businesses and farmers. Antonio had also donated thousands more to provide shade along the roads and was encouraging his neighbours to plant native species by throwing in a few seedlings for free when they came to buy eucalyptus. Growing to maturity in about three or four years, the trees had become a kind of bank for the settlers. "If I need to buy a new tire for my car, some shoes for my wife, I don't have to sell a cow or a sheep if the prices are low," he explained. "I can cut down a few trees, and sell the lumber." Prices were high: All kinds of local industries, from brick works to pizza parlours, depended on firewood for fuel, and thanks to the ranching, the settlers and their stands of eucalyptus were one of the few sources available to them.

Since college-level agronomy courses that taught organic methods were impossible to find, the MST had, by 2006, founded two agro-ecology schools of their own. The most recently inaugurated was that of Itapeva, where Roberval worked. There, the usual political slogans now went like this: "We fight agribusiness every day — with the agro-ecology of the MST!" Thirty young students, the children of settlers and camp dwellers, were just finishing up the first phase of their training course, an occasion marked by songs, a *mistica* — a slightly awkward yet ultimately touching theatrical presentation on the nineteen MST comrades murdered in Para — and a massive barbecue. According to Jose Batista in São Paulo, for the MST, ecologically responsible farming was "an essential strategy. That's the phase we are in today," he said, "not only guaranteeing our existence but a production based on our values. What we are doing is constructing a whole new form of production."

"Fighting agribusiness" is a relatively new front for the movement, despite the fact that over the past decades, landless peasants often occupied and de-manded the expropriation of estates belonging to individuals or companies involved in it. Throughout the organization, people were also realizing that traditional peasant farming is almost always in danger of being crushed by what one member called "the multinational agro-industrial food com-plex." This complex has grown increasingly powerful — and problematic — in today's world. Companies like Cargill, the largest privately owned corporation in the United States, and Archer Daniels Midland, control 45 percent and 30 percent of the world's grain trade, respectively. They, along with companies like Monsanto, Syngenta, Dupont, Dow, Bayer and BASF either cultivate huge expanses of land or sell chemicals and genetically modified seeds to their growing global customer base, feeding their addiction and harming waterways and wildlife. As their products fill supermarkets across the globe — Cargill, for example, is the largest processor of beef in Canada — they also receive major hand-outs from the public purse. Moreover, the excess from these subsidized producers is often sent as food aid to poor countries by U.S., Canadian and European governments, earning them even more profits. And companies like Cargill and ADM have taken increasing advantage of their superior financial and logistical leads, imposing cut-throat pricing on small farmers or leaving them out of the picture all together, as developing countries comply with international trade regulations and dismantle their farm marketing boards.

In Brazil, two other sectors further promise to skew land distribution, destroy natural environments and ratchet up rural poverty. The bio-fuel pact signed by Luiz Inácio "Lula" da Silva and president George W. Bush in March 2007 brought with it the spectre of vast acreages, including those in the Amazon, being planted in sugar cane. Meanwhile, the global demand for items as innocuous as tissue paper has made a company like Aracruz Celulose S.A. the world's largest producer of pulp made from bleached eucalyptus, responsible for one quarter overall of the global supply, along with multi-millions in profit.

The extraordinary concentration of basic commodities in the hands of a few has at least one major foe, however, in La Vía Campesina. Founded in 1992, this international movement of small landholders represents more than 170 organizations in countries around the world, including Canada's National Farmers Union. Saturnino Borras, the Canada Research Chair in International Development Studies at Saint Mary's University in Halifax, has described the agendas and demands of La Vía Campesina as constituting "a serious counter-argument to the neo-liberal doctrine," exemplified by the political and economic opportunities offered these agribusiness behemoths, and "a veritable alternative 'voice' from below, representing marginalized rural peoples in the world."

An international counterweight to the threat of new business realities has become more crucial than ever. The blatantly skewed distribution of farmland is a hallmark of many developing nations and a clear contributor to the vast scale of poverty within them. In the Philippines, where a land reform plan enacted during the presidency of Cory Aquino left many large estates, including that of her family, intact, there are four million landless or land poor peasants — about 80 percent of the agricultural population. Thailand, according to the FAO, has 2.1 million land poor and more than 700,000 rural labourers. In Pakistan, 3.8 million peasant families till plots of less than two hectares yet account for one half of all agricultural holdings.

In South Africa, meanwhile, by the end of the apartheid regime white farmers owned 88 percent of its arable land. Yet, the African National Congress government has managed to lower that amount by only 3 percent — after promising 30 percent in its 1994 Reconstruction and Development Programme — and has halted any further attempts to distribute land to the nation's majority black farmers.

In Central America, land reform has also been the focal point of often-violent local struggle. In Guatemala, for example, 90 percent of the rural population lives in poverty, while less than 1 percent of landowners possess 75 percent of its best agricultural land. Honduras has equally lop-sided land ownership. There, 62 percent of the land belongs to farmers with 50 hectares or more. Yet they make up only 10 percent of all holdings, while peasant farmers with less than five hectares make up 72 percent of all holdings and own just 7 percent of the land. It is not surprising that nations like

Honduras are thus major exporters of cheap labour to countries like Canada and the United States. By now, remittances from abroad account for more than a quarter of Honduras's GDP. Yet the question of fair land ownership in the Third World remains a controversial subject few if any development economists and aid providers will take on.

What's more, advocates of agrarian reform must now contend with an alarming new trend as corporations, agribusiness, investment banks, hedge funds and commodity traders quietly buy up or lease immense tracts of land in some of the world's poorest nations. Tens of thousands of hectares in size, they are being used to cultivate food, palm oil, eucalyptus — even flowers — for export directly back to their far more lucrative home markets. Private firms from Saudi Arabia, Kuwait, Qatar, Japan and even China are carving out these estates in some of the very countries listed above — as well as Chad, Sudan, Zimbabwe, Kenya, Indonesia, Brazil and Cambodia. Laos has reportedly signed away 15 percent of its arable land to foreign companies from China, Japan and Sweden. The two million hectares purchased in Pakistan by Saudi and other companies even come with a 100,000-man private army. And in Ethiopia, where almost six million families own one hectare or less, another 2.1 million are landless and 13 million people receive food aid, Saudi investors are paying billions for land on which to grow vegetables, wheat and barley for export. While this defies all moral and common sense, it is entirely in keeping with capitalist logic.

As part of La Vía Campesina and in keeping with its own political philosophy, the MST has led or joined various campaigns against agribusiness. Some take place on the international stage, but many — because of Brazil's economic clout and unequal wealth — find numerous examples at home. One successful struggle involved the reclaiming of more than 10,000 hectares of land taken by Aracruz from the indigenous Tupinikim and Guarani peoples in the state of Espiritu Santo.

In 1970, there were forty Tupinikim villages in the area from which the company was to take its name. During the military dictatorship, with the support of municipal, state and federal governments and through a variety of means, the company was able to appropriate more than 40,000 hectares in all, leaving only forty for its previous inhabitants. In this way, Aracruz became the state's single biggest landowner. Their vast holding was planted entirely with eucalyptus, in this case a species that not only excretes an acid into the soil that kills anything growing nearby but hogs massive amounts of groundwater.

During both the 2002 and 2006 presidential campaigns, Aracruz reportedly provided hefty financial support to the Workers Party. A year after Luiz Inácio da Silva's first election in 2002, the corporation won a loan worth over half a billion dollars from the government-run National Bank for Economic and Social Development, or BNDES. Even more crucially perhaps, the Workers Party government joined previous administrations in refusing to return the land taken from the Tupinikim in Espiritu Santo, territory they wanted back.

In 2005, about a hundred Tupinikim families began to occupy the land, but they were violently expelled by federal police and Aracruz employees the following year. Two months later, as Da Silva welcomed guests to the United Nations–sponsored Conference on Agrarian Reform and Rural Development in Porto Alegre, two thousand La Vía Campesina activists entered Aracruz's laboratory in Barra do Ribeiro, Rio Grande do Sul, and uprooted more than a million eucalyptus seedlings. Thirty-eight people were charged for the action, which, according to Isabella Kenfield, "demonstrated the emerging alliance between Brazilian indigenous movements and those united under La Vía Campesina, an alliance that strengthened after the police raid in Espiritu Santo."

Two weeks later, La Vía Campesina members also occupied an experimental site belonging to Swiss company, Syngenta, in Parana. The Tupinikim and Guarani meanwhile renewed their struggle to win back their territory, reconstructing villages and burning down several hundred hectares of eucalyptus. Together with some five hundred MST activists, they also occupied the seaport Aracruz shares with Cenibra, a Brazilian-Japanese consortium, losing them an estimated $21 million, according to Kenfield. While the scale of protest, the international outcry and the determination shown by the indigenous and grassroots movements in solidarity with them finally forced the minister of justice, Tarso Genro, to demarcate the area in their favour, this long-contested land, like that ceded to the Camargo family in Pontal de Paranapanema, was exhausted by the extraordinary toll the trees have taken on it.

The Aracruz campaign illustrates another aspect of the MST: its relationship with the Workers Party government. In many ways, the MST's autonomous stance has important implications for grassroots social movements all over the world as they deal, inevitably, with the issue of electoral politics. When it was first formed in 1979, the Partido dos Trabalhadores, or Workers Party, represented a breakthrough for the left of almost heady proportions, the recovery of militancy by a working class pounded by the country's military dictatorship and business elite. With its origins in radical unionism, a *nordestino* migrant metal worker as its leader, socialism as its aim and a political platform that took on the vindications of workers and other oppressed groups in the largest country in Latin America, its emergence rescued many from the notion that working-class politics were either outdated or moribund. The Workers Party and what it stood for seemed to counter everything that was wrong with the old Brazil: its exploitative wages and great swathes of poverty, its wanton destruction of its environment in the name of profit, its violence and the corruption at the heart of its politics.

In championing the need to overturn the country's unfair system of land ownership, the Workers Party openly sympathized with the plight of the landless and supported their struggles. Settlers in the *agro-vilas* also found it much easier to deal with local and state Workers Party governors than previous ones and were often able to prosper because of it. In return, the MST was largely supportive of the Workers Party's electoral aims — although as early as April 2001, an MST representative criticized the party at the Quebec City Summit of the Americas — and considered it the only one capable of being elected and thus beginning their promised transformation of Brazilian society. Yet it has proven to be vital to its success that the fortunes of the MST do not rise and fall with those of the Workers Party.

According to Sue Branford, the great trust placed in the Workers Party by rank-and-file members was a problem for the MST. "The rural poor," she wrote in a Latin America Bureau report, "were jubilant when Lula was elected president. Tens of thousands of families joined the movement and squatted on the verges of federal highways, confident that Lula would honour his earlier pledge to the MST 'to give you so much land that you will not know what to do with it.' The MST leadership, however, was wary from the start, turning down Lula's repeated offers of top jobs for MST leaders.... On several occasions," Branford added, "militants organized marches on Brasilia in support of the movement's radical demands, only to have Lula come down from the Presidential Palace and speak directly to the marchers in his charismatic way. On one memorable occasion, Lula doffed the MST's characteristic red cap and spoke to the march. 'You have waited for 500 years to see a working-class man in the Presidency of Brazil,' he said. 'But I can't achieve everything you want in just a few years. And I beg you to be patient.' Lula was applauded at the end of his address (to the evident discomfort of some of the militants)."

The Workers Party, however, was only able to gain power through coalitions with other parties that did not share its stated political aims, and this has been the excuse for certainly the first term's abandoning its radical positions. Clearly, however, with the re-election of da Silva in 2006 and the victory of his former chief of staff, Dilma Roussef, in October 2010, there is no longer any possibility of justifying the Workers Party government's hearty embrace of neo-liberal, pro-capitalist policies, of favouring the rich with their BNDES loans over the poor and their monthly Bolsa Familia handouts.

Just like its appalling failure to defend the Amazon rain forest, the Workers Party government has turned out to be as unwilling to deliver meaningful land reform as its predecessors. In a 2004 article, João Pedro Stedile commented on the months of debate the MST held with the new government in an attempt to elaborate an effective agrarian reform plan. "There were sectors… that wanted to provide land to only 80,000 families in the three upcoming years," he wrote. "And there was a team from the Ministry of Agrarian Reform that planned the possibility of settling a million families in four years. We thus came to an agreement with respect to the goals for the next three years in which the government committed itself to settle 400,000 families." And yet, he added, this agreement was one that existed only on paper and has never materialized.

The movement's response to the lack of action came in April 2004, when it launched a national campaign in a surge of pressure, occupying 150 estates and setting up camps with 200,000 families. Like the battles against eucalyptus monocultures, it has mounted various, highly visible protests against the government and its new elite allies. The once affable Lula with his working-class roots and *nordestino* accent, once so mocked in the right-wing media, was no longer invited to MST national congresses. In 2005, movement members marched through the streets of Brasilia with banners accusing the government of "impeding agrarian reform." The implication that progressive political parties and grassroots social movements can have conflicting agendas is unmistakable. Like a hug from a boa constrictor, envelopment by such parties can spell death.

This has been amply demonstrated in the history of another social movement, the Confederation of Indigenous Nationalities of Ecuador. Over the years since its founding in 1986, the CONAIE succeeded in mobilizing hundreds of thousands of poor and marginalized indigenous from fourteen different ethnic groups to fight for various rights, including the resources of their territories. A decade later, it reversed its negative view of party politics by joining with other social justice groups in forming their own party, called Pachakutik. As a front of resistance to Ecuador's corrupt and undemocratic system, it instigated four major uprisings and brought down the government of president Jamil Muhuad early in the year 2000. It then, however, formed an electoral alliance with Lucio Gutiérrez, an army colonel who considered himself a leftist in the mould of Hugo Chávez. According to Scott Beck, co-author of *New Age, Old Politics: The Rise and Decline of the Ecuadorean Indigenous Movement*, the colonel "certainly talked up indigenous autonomy and agrarian reform, various things that were in line with the CONAIE program."

Although many of CONAIE's militants were promised — and given — posts in Gutiérrez's new "National Salvation Government," their involvement seems to have driven a wedge between the organization's leaders and those on the ground. "In Bolivar province," said Beck, "we've had a couple of militants tell us that in 2001, they had this assembly to decide whether they should back Gutiérrez or go with another candidate or not back anybody for president. They'd actually decided they didn't want to support Gutiérrez, but the national representative from CONAIE who was there, went back and lied, and said they had supported backing (him). They felt manipulated and used, and still resented that in 2006."

Within six months of his election, Gutiérrez abandoned his progressive pledges and embraced typical neo-liberal economic policies; his indigenous supporters left in disgust. Yet, said Beck, "the indigenous movement really suffered seriously for a while after that, and some would say they never really recovered." What's more, "Lucio Gutiérrez did everything he could to weaken, divide and destroy the indigenous movement, especially CONAIE," he added, "and he did a pretty good job of it." The 2006 elections "were an embarrassment" for CONAIE and Pachakutik, which won only 2 percent of the vote.

The entire episode raises questions concerning "the relationship between social movements pressing for significant if not radical social and economic changes, and political parties that may in some ways seek their support and want to grab some of the energy from these social movements," Beck said, "and how those kinds of things turn out, both in the short and the long run." In the case of the CONAIE, that relationship left it devastated.

For the MST, their independence from the Workers Party has also been a question of balance. Certainly, there is still a convergence of empathy within both, as many in the Workers Party's own rank and file are unhappy with the way the long-sought grail of governing Brazil has turned out. Yet the MST must nonetheless deal with the state as it is now embodied by the Workers Party, and this implies a series of challenges. How to relate to a political force with which it once shared common goals and features? How to avoid co-optation — the tempting possibility of a few government positions in return for cooling the criticism? Or, on the opposite end of the spectrum, how to avert demoralization among members as they quickly learn that they are still at the bottom of the heap in the eyes of da Silva's — and now Roussef's — administration?

In this case, keeping its focus on local, autonomous activity as the real route to change has served to consolidate the movement's forces. By continuing to organize large, simultaneous land occupations throughout the country, the MST, in the words of Stedile, "is defending the urgency and necessity of recovering grassroots working methods, that is, to concentrate on small tasks; to go to where people live, work and study to debate ideas and organize them."

Striking the right balance — between the movement and the state, the national and the local, even between the struggles to own a piece of land and to make a living from it — is complex, yet a crucial aspect of the movement's future. As they define their relationships with political parties of the left, grassroots social movements around the world will have to consider these questions.

Autonomy is an important factor in the success of grassroots social movements not only in their relationships with other players, but also in the material sense. The viability of any grassroots social movement — but particularly one that is run by the poor — is often closely tied to the ability to lay its hands on resources. Communications, travel, educational material, the training, salaries and office expenses of activists all require money. This almost always implies donations from other organizations sympathetic to their cause, either in the country where they operate or abroad. However, their need can leave them potentially vulnerable to the influence of those who control this funding, to churches, international development agencies or NGOs, organizations whose members and donors may not always agree with radical and antagonistic attitudes towards authorities, property rights or the rule of law. The danger of diluting local demands, of curbing them to fit international agendas, or of censoring activity to make the organization more acceptable to external sponsors, is always hovering on the sidelines of the search for donor funding.

This search can, moreover, drain away the attention to activism, even make it altogether detrimental, as members feel constrained to work in ways that are acceptable to their external sponsors.

Nonetheless, it only follows that the more successful a movement is — the better its track record in achieving concrete gains and making projects work — the easier it can be for them to attract attention and support from external funding bodies. What's more, the emphasis on economic wellbeing and growth can allow them to generate more income internally and eventually, move towards self-sustainability, leaving donor dollars for other movements of the poor.

In the case of the MST, its members provide the basic financial underpinning of the movement as a whole. A percentage of the INCRA credits — originally 2 percent and now 3 — paid out once estate land has been expropriated and divided up, goes to its National Association of Agricultural Cooperation, or ANCA. These funds are used to offset a number of expenditures, including help for those still struggling for land in the encampments. While the organization refused to confirm the claim at the time, an article in *Time* magazine from 1998 suggested that its annual budget amounted to the surprisingly high figure of $120 million.

However Igor Santos of the MST's communications section in São Paulo stressed that, in an organization that is highly decentralized, it is virtually impossible to say what such a figure might amount to. "With militants in 24 states," he said, "the MST is very large and dynamic. It's not like a business." The states and regions themselves, he added, raise funds on their own, destined for particular projects. They also frequently partner with both domestic and international organizations on such projects. Brazilian society has been especially supportive, he pointed out, in recognizing the need for agrarian reform and sympathizing with the struggles of the poor to achieve it.

The material prosperity of someone like Antonio Camargo, as well as that of the MST members who have formed cooperatives, actually strengthens the argument for agrarian reform in the developing world. For critics of agrarian reform, the financial and production difficulties faced by peasants "given" land by the state are the inevitable onslaughts of a losing battle. The greater efficiencies and productivity of large-scale, mechanized farming, they say, make it the ideal contender in the war against global hunger. Never mind the long-term costs — environmental damage, concentration of resources and ensuing urban poverty — the superior logistics of corporate agribusiness justify all of this, not to mention the financial incentives it gets from public and private sources alike.

While peasant-based and family agriculture is severely challenged by such competition and the entire macro-economic climate in Brazil, as well as in pretty much every low-income country, the MST tries to counter this model through its Confederation of Agrarian Reform Cooperatives, or CONCRAB. As the movement encourages settlements to form cooperatives and receive better pricing by cutting out the market's intermediaries, CONCRAB goes much further by providing free technical advice and training. Indeed an evaluation of its Program of Accompaniment of Social Enterprises explained how government resources for rural families are not only inadequate but often unavailable when they are needed and can be most effective. "Essential services, such as technical assistance, education and training, basic health care, transport and so on, are forgotten or discontinued," it adds, "contributing to the lack of stimulation and the abandonment of lots by families."

The staff at CONCRAB, many of them children of original MST settlers, offer advice on everything from better agricultural methods and reforestation to marketing strategies and administration. According to Alexandre Rangel, they work with 362 cooperatives and social enterprises. Among the most prominent are Coopavi, a Parana-based producer and exporter of sugar cane derivatives, and Cooperoeste in Santa Catarina, which markets 180,000 litres of milk every month, as well as canned vegetables, under the Terra Viva brand name; 6000 families participate in the large cooperative that, as its website declares, "was created with the objective of offering people the opportunity for a more dignified life." Meanwhile, the members of Coopat in Rio Grande do Sul went from earning low prices for their organic rice to processing and packaging 250 tonnes a year for direct sale. Each of these cooperative businesses currently does over $1 million in sales annually. As with the occupations of the landless to win land, organization and education constitute an alternative to rural poverty from below, building what the Confederation has described as "greater levels of resistance to the advances of the capitalist dynamic."

While the productivity and financial success of these collective enterprises offer an example of the inherent logic of land reform and poverty reduction, the MST has also begun to occupy and set up what it calls land communes right on the outskirts of mega-cities like São Paulo. Offering a new way of life to the urban poor, the commune plots are only a few hectares in size but have the potential of producing healthier, cheaper food than that found in supermarkets just a few minutes away.

This entrepreneurial feature of the MST, while controversial, is another illustration of the ability of the poor to remake their economic reality when given the basic means to do so. Even as it invites criticism from the right for being less efficient than traditional business, by maintaining a system of private land ownership and working within the current capitalist system to market products, it leaves some on the left uncomfortable. Yet as the influx of rural poor to big cities exemplifies, in order for capitalism to flourish it needs to create a large and steady pool of labourers prepared to take low wages in order to have work, people who will do anything to survive. It has proven itself adept, especially in the developing world, at depriving the poor of the possibility of economically empowering themselves. The financial success of the MST cooperatives show, in turn, how once the tools of empowerment, such as land, are grasped, people previously excluded from all but the least rewarding of economic activity are suddenly able to flourish, innovate and compete with the system as participants in an economy of solidarity. The enterprises built by the poor, therefore, represent the logical outcome of the organized struggle to escape poverty.

By now, the narrative of the MST is filled with personal anecdotes of economic transformation. Because of their organizing and activism, hundreds of thousands of people who began their lives facing bleak futures of illiteracy, social rejection and wearisome, low-paid labour, now plant and harvest their own crops. They are running cooperatives, packing plants and schools. What is significant is that this transformation has not alienated them from the practices of solidarity needed for the struggle. On the contrary, MST settlers, no longer landless, remain MST members, with a strong sense of identity with the movement and its long-term goals and a desire to see others once like them given the same chance to succeed. As Jose Batista put it, "While there is still no real land reform in Brazil, we are all *sem terra*."

For Paulo Barros da Silva and his wife Maria the possibility of beginning new lives as independent and productive farmers was, in the end, not to come until the end of 2010. Along with their comrades, they spent more than four years living in a roadside camp in front of the land on which Paulo had worked, "trying to get some food together for the kids," and where Maria had raised her guinea hens. So why did a process that began with the Institute for Colonization and Agrarian Reform admitting that Fazenda Juá was ripe for expropriation take so long?

Part of the problem lay in the very geography of its 5500 hectares of *sertão*. It turned out that the MST were not the only ones eyeing Fazenda Juá: environmental authorities had also decided to expropriate most of it in order to enlarge and consolidate the Serra do Catimbau National Park. This meant that two different government departments — the Brazilian Institute for the Environment and the Chico Mendes Institute for Biodiversity that replaced it in 2008 — had to evaluate the impact of distributing the remaining land. Moving at a pace that would have put the rubber tapper activist for which it was named to shame, it took more than a year and a half to do so. And while it finally decided in January 2010 that the area outside the park could be farmed without harming its environment, the INCRA took another ten months to complete yet another inspection and decide the terms of the expropriation.

For Paulo Barros da Silva, the Correia family, Alexandre and Lucia and the rest, the quest for land proved as arduous, dangerous and frustrating as so many others in the history of the MST. Yet they have finally become what the National Slum Dwellers Federation in India calls "part of the big," their role in the collective struggle a vehicle that has taken them from poverty to that long-sought "opportunity for a more dignified life." The future will no doubt continue to present them with new tests and trials, but the ongoing search for grassroots solutions to them will inevitably be a natural outcome of what had to be done to win their land in the first place.

Part 2

Indonesia

• 3 •

A Walk in the Woods

Like most of the forest peasants in the village of Rimpak, Kito Haryanto goes into the jungle near his house just about every day to search for something: fallen wood for the kitchen fire, animal forage, wild spinach or the mushrooms that suddenly appear during rainy season. On one Sunday in mid-July 2008, however, he makes an exception. He walks instead to the house of Rimpak's former headman, Suyoto, for a meeting about a new problem — one that could keep him out of the forest for good.

Kito has little land to plant, less than a hectare, but enough for himself, his wife Wariyanti and their two small children. With careful cultivation and sufficient rain, he gets plenty of sweet potatoes, cassava, cabbages, onions, bananas and maize, which when ground and cooked is called "corn-rice" by the local peasants. Although they much prefer the real thing, rice is about the only crop Kito cannot grow. His scattered farm plots are also in the forest, in what in Indonesia is known as productive forest. Set within its hilly terrain and laid out in neat rows, these are surrounded by, or even dotted with, pines and albasia trees. Even the village of Rimpak is itself steeply pitched, two rows of simple brick houses, each pair terraced above those below, with a narrow cement walk rising between them.

And like almost all the peasant households there, half of the Haryanto family income comes from the baskets and woven rice bowls Kito and his wife make and sell in the market of the nearest city, Wonosobo. For these he needs the forest and its lush feathery groves of green bamboo. He heads out every five days, he says, for another supply of stalks, which he then cuts into thin strips to dry. It takes a day to complete two small baskets, "working from 7 a.m. to 7 p.m.," he specifies. Once he has enough to sell, he and Wariyanti spend half the night carrying them by foot eight kilometres to the highway, using torches to illuminate the rock-strewn dirt road winding down out of the village. They earn the equivalent of about fifty cents each for large baskets and less than half of that for the small ones. Yet they represent the couple's main source of hard cash, money for real rice, oil, clothing and shoes, to pay six-year-old Tikno's primary school fees and the local medicine woman, who helped eight months earlier with the birth of their baby daughter Ri'fah.

Compared to Suyoto's house, with its smoked plate-glass front window and ample collection of upholstered chairs, settees and coffee tables, Kito's is very plain. The cement plaster on its brick walls hasn't seen a new coat of blue paint in many years; beneath the tile roof, a blackened, cobwebby loft is only partly ceilinged off. The front room, its cement floor covered with thin mats, is bare but for an ancient television set and a few plastic toys.

Now, along with several hundred others, Kito has been told that if he continues to enter the forest, he'll face a fine of five billion rupiah, about $50,000, and/or a jail sentence of up to ten years. The company making that threat is called Perum Perhutani, a state-owned corporation commercializing wood furniture and other forest products, such as resin from the pine trees around Kito's plot. Perhutani has the concession to the forest around Rimpak and across much of the municipality of Wonosobo, almost 19,000 hectares. And while the company asserts that its natural resins, oils, lumber and other raw materials are the products of sustainable harvesting that doesn't harm the ecological balance of the forest, it lost its international certification a few years ago because of the various social conflicts in which it has been involved.

How can one company impose such a drastic intervention in the lives of the peasants who live here? The answer is embedded in a complicated series of elements, in Indonesia's geography, its history and its politics since independence from Holland in 1945.

Almost half of Indonesia's great archipelago is still covered in tropical forests, home to an extraordinary diversity of trees, plant species and exotic wildlife such as rhinoceros, tigers, leopards and orangutans. Yet this fact poses a unique problem for millions of rural families.

As in Brazil, land ownership in Indonesia is highly concentrated, with 70 percent of farmers owning just 13 percent of the arable land, much of it in plots of one hectare or less. Large estate-holders and corporations, both national and international, cultivate the remainder, while more than 13 million rural workers are landless. This pattern, inherited from Indonesia's European colonizers and exacerbated during the authoritarian regime of Suharto, helps endow the fourth most populous country in the world with one of the highest poverty rates in Southeast Asia.

But the largest landowner of them all is the Ministry of Forestry. A decree passed in the early years of Suharto's self-serving reign placed all forested and fallow lands under state control. In fact, this gives the state effective decision-making power over more than 70 percent of Indonesia's landmass, more than 100 million hectares by some estimates. The Ministry of Forestry also has the right to identify what is forest as opposed to agricultural land. Since the 1967 law doesn't recognize the *adat*, or customary rights, of the communities who have lived in and from the forest for centuries, it has transformed as many as 60 million people into illegal squatters. According to Monica Di

Gregorio of the London School of Economics and Political Science, "The lack of recognition of customary rights has thus increased landlessness and land conflicts, and has reduced tenure security for millions of rural villagers. These conditions have resulted in increased disenfranchisement, marginalisation, impoverishment and vulnerability of people living in the forest margins, as well as massive deforestation and environmental degradation."

The nation's constitution gives the state the right to control its forests — sub-divided into four different types — and exploit them "to the greatest benefit of the people." But in reality, this has been interpreted as the right to misuse natural resources in the interests of a small and very wealthy percentage of the population. Under Suharto, "the greatest benefit of the people" was defined as his own, that of his family, the military bigwigs who supported him and their assorted cronies and friends. Over the thirty-two years of his rule, hundreds of concessions were handed out for tourism projects, plantations, logging and mining, even in areas deemed protected or conservation forests. By 1990, the Suharto government had authorized logging on almost 58 million hectares of forest. While these brought millions in profits to multinational corporations, the army and corrupt government officials, as Di Gregorio has pointed out, they also destroyed forest cover, polluted waterways and took away the homes and livelihoods of indigenous and forest villagers. Indonesia, moreover, now has the longest list of endangered animal species in the world.

While the struggle for agrarian reform in Indonesia in many ways reflects that of Brazil's rural poor, current forest tenure policies mean that significant amounts of land without tree cover — about 40 percent of the Ministry of Forestry's holdings — can never be considered for reallocation to smallholding peasant farmers. The 1967 law makes a very clear, if artificial, distinction between the two, farmland and forest land — and with the nation's constitution.

Indonesia's Basic Agrarian Law of 1960 was a reaction to the unjust land distribution practices of the Dutch and the poverty they created. Its relevant articles state that every Indonesian, men and women, has the right to own land and enjoy its benefits. It also recognizes *adat* rights of tenure. And Article 10 even goes so far as to stipulate that persons or companies with a right to agricultural land are obliged to actively till the land themselves. Little wonder then, that the later forestry law has been so important to the state in blocking such principles — and put forestry right at the heart of most agrarian struggles in Indonesia today.

For even with the ouster of Suharto in 1998, the policies of successive democratically elected governments still leave forest dwellers at a marked disadvantage. An integral part of its economic development plans for attracting foreign investment and helping national companies compete in the global marketplace, the Indonesian state still considers the nation's natural resources an important cash cow. "There has been no change before or after the fall of Suharto," said Hein Mallee, a specialist with Canada's International Development Research Centre in Singapore. With project managers and researchers told from the outset that tenure rights are not up for discussion under any circumstances, he said, "it's a political issue; it's a very sensitive one, and on full ownership there hasn't been any progress for decades."

Meanwhile, along with the 1997 economic crisis and other factors, the loosening of political restrictions and government decentralization have helped create a decade-long boom in illegal logging. The laws on decentralization were conceived and passed very quickly in 1999, leaving as many conflicting regulations and murky practices as it has regrets on the part of Indonesia's central government in Jakarta. With district leaders feeling free to hand out concessions to private companies for timber or plantations in areas of protected forest (often in return for personal gain), many suspect that the corruption has simply fanned out from the central level to regional ones. Mallee sees it as more complicated than that. "There is an enormous proliferation of all kinds of rules," he explained, "but really, who can do what in a particular situation isn't very clear at all." And, he added, "Corruption and power plays thrive in a situation where there is a lack of clarity about the rules. Having power, you can manipulate, you can create new rules."

The result is a staggering amount of forest loss — as much as two million hectares annually, by most estimates, or ten acres every minute. In 1997 and 1998, more than five million hectares of logged over timber concessions were burned, most of it by companies hoping to convert them into oil palm or other types of plantations. Yet government bureaucrats and corporate exploiters of the forest, such as Perhutani, often blame forest peasants for deforestation. They consider them encroachers or worse: as aiders and abettors of criminal gangs that plunder precious resources and cause environmental havoc. Or perhaps it is simpler to blame the poor, who have little if any defence. What is clear is that the priorities of both government and corporations have to do with stemming logging by illegal competitors and enhancing the bottom line, rather than dealing with tenure issues.

Yet as Ismail, headman in nearby Tanjuang-Anon village and a supporter of forest peasant rights, put it: "The peasants have created a kind of mutual relationship with nature. It is very difficult for them to survive without the forest — and very difficult for the forest to survive without them."

Throughout Indonesia, increasing numbers of indigenous peoples and forest peasants have embraced this view. Among them are the villagers of Rimpak. Over the glasses of sugared tea and plates of biscuits, the discussion at Suyoto's house lengthens. Even as the mechanical clock in a corner bookcase sounds out the *azaan* call to prayer, no one pays attention, intent as everyone is on expressing the centrality of this great natural resource to their lives. "Yes, the forest land belongs to the government," says Kito, "but since the time of our ancestors, we have been doing what we do, gathering foods and bamboo to make our living. We have been doing that to survive."

It is damp and chilly up here in Java's highlands, so Kito wears a black quilted jacket over his white shirt and trousers, a white knitted kufi cap over his thick straight hair. He's come to the meeting with his neighbours, Munah Mai, a jovial young woman wearing a hijab, and Rahyono, a thin, dark man with a sad, patient aspect, quietly smoking clove cigarettes while Kito does most of the talking.

None of them understands why exactly Perhutani has prohibited them from going into the forest or is accusing the forest peasants of destroying it. Not only do villagers lack the equipment to cut and transport timber, they are only interested, they argue, in harvesting the jungle for useful things and cropping beneath the tree cover.

Nine years earlier, says Kito, renegade loggers came in and started illegally cutting down mature trees, a practice that, in total, reduced Perhutani's standing stock alone by 4 percent in just one year. But he adds, "We're pretty sure there is no more illegal logging nowadays, because the peasants also inhabit the forest. If it were going on, we would know. We would see it right away, and we would be very angry. And we would go there collectively, and that's why the illegal loggers are afraid of the peasants. And that's why we think it would be much safer, and even more profitable, if the peasants manage the forest, because we don't destroy it and we also have this sort of supervising system, which couldn't be done by Perhutani. Even now, in several places where we are not allowed to get in, we don't know for sure whether there are any activities of illegal logging or not. Because Perhutani doesn't pay much attention, while we go there every day and we look after the trees. If there was even a slight difference or damage, we would know that something was wrong."

In fact, interjects Suyoto, Perhutani itself has less respect for the forest than the peasants. "One time," he says, "they had a plan to cut down all the bamboo, something that would cause soil erosion and landslides." The company had already replaced the groves of albasia and other species with pine.

"This endangers the peasants," Kito maintains, "because pine absorbs more water and that causes a diminishing number of springs in our area. Where the forest had albasia trees and not pine, we could endure a nine-month period with no rain, because we still had lots of water, but now we can only endure about two months."

Shortly after the first trespass warnings came from a local police officer named Marino, employed by Perhutani to carry out its orders, a number of forest peasants travelled to Wonosobo to ask for help at the local office of the Serikat Petani, or Peasants' Union, of Indonesia. There they met with its provincial leader, Somairi, a thoughtful, soft-spoken man of thirty-nine, whose methodical manner of speech has a way of giving rise to a certain amount of good-natured teasing from his SPI comrades. More often than not sleeping on a quilted mat on the office floor instead of at home, living on tea, coffee and his endless clove cigarettes, Somairi has a look about him of permanent weariness, his face in need of a shave and his long-sleeved shirt of a pressing. He is a man for whom the struggle is all consuming, and patience not so much a virtue as a necessity in a nation like Indonesia.

Together he and the peasants went to the local House of Representatives to expose Perhutani's denial of forest access and, as Kito puts it, "to negotiate." Indeed, there is no quick fix to the challenge posed by the company and the laws that give it such formidable powers. As dates get set for more meetings and municipal authorities figure out who should have representation at them, Somairi and the villagers of Rimpak have come up with a new idea. Because of their many conflicts with peasants in other parts of Java over forested lands, Perhutani has had many run-ins over the past decade with the SPI, the leading movement for agrarian reform in Indonesia. Somairi therefore believes they will get further with a slightly different strategy. So the villagers of Rimpak have formed a new branch, the Forest Peasants Group, affiliated to the SPI.

Over the following weeks, the SPI quickly began a campaign to educate the peasants about their rights and, even more urgently, to persuade them to resist signing a Perhutani-created document agreeing to never enter the forest again. For in spite of an agreement between the Forest Peasants Group and the House of Representatives allowing forest peasants to carry on as before while talks are being set up, hundreds of these documents were brought round to Rimpak and six other villages. "Even after this was signed, Officer Marino still kept coming here and intimidating peasants to sign the other agreement," complains Suyoto. While in Waranang, the hamlet where Rahyono lives, "people are still too scared to go into the forest right now," he admits, the majority were defying the corporation's threats. In Rimpak alone, only fifteen of its 300 households were pressured into signing.

Kito sees two important advantages in joining the SPI. In an area where there have been sporadic conflicts in the past, he points out, uniting the villages in their demand to retain their right of access is one. The other, however, is its emphasis on education. "Before the SPI came, I didn't really know what was going on," he says. "I am not well-educated, only primary school, so I don't have much knowledge about things." As part of the movement, forest peasants were suddenly talking about their rights, the nation's laws and better farming methods. "Of course," he adds, "we basically want a better economy and more development, but we cannot get these without being given the right to manage the forest products."

Primarily an agrarian movement based on the vindication of the rights of the peasant class, the SPI first came together as a federation of regional peasant unions in 1998. Through protest, struggle and negotiation, its 700,000 members have since won or reclaimed a million hectares of land from big plantation owners cultivating rubber, tea, palm oil and other commodities. Today, the similar assertion of the nation's forests for the poor who have traditionally depended on their resources represents a new, and still relatively small, front of action. However the movement's integration of a rights-based perspective into entrenched notions of environmental conservation has generated a valuable and far more democratic approach to the issue. For many classic conservation movements, based and funded in affluent countries, this is very much at odds with their vision of saving the world's endangered forestlands.

In his book *Conservation Refugees: The Hundred-Year Conflict Between Global Conservation and Native Peoples*, investigative journalist Mark Dowie illuminates this discrepancy in stark terms. He chronicles a heart-rending series of evictions of communities from the forests where they had lived sustainably for centuries, reduced to poverty and even extinction, as a result of typical environmental campaigning. "It's no secret that millions of native peoples around the world have been pushed off their land to make room for big oil, big metal, big timber, and big agriculture," Dowie wrote in an earlier article. "But few people realize that the same thing has happened for a much nobler cause: land and wildlife conservation. Today the list of culture-wrecking institutions put forth by tribal leaders on almost every continent includes not only Shell, Texaco, Freeport, and Bechtel, but also more surprising names like Conservation International, The Nature Conservancy, the World Wildlife Fund, and the Wildlife Conservation Society. Even the more culturally sensitive World Conservation Union might get a mention."

Dowie reveals how Big Conservation has created millions — more than 14 million in Africa alone, according to Cornell University's Charles Geisler — of poor and financially dependent people. Out of the 108,000 areas given official protection worldwide since 1910, more than half were occupied or used by forest dwellers. Thus, as indigenous and forest dwellers increasingly see the activities of conservation organizations as a massive threat, conservationists see them, in turn, as complicit in the loss of bio-diversity.

Yet many documented studies show that forest peasants are in fact very often able to live in harmony with their unique habitat. Depending on the extension of forest in which they live, areas may be cultivated for as little as two years, then left fallow for as many as sixty. Others harvest products from the trees and other naturally occurring species for their livelihood, leaving certain trees and planting new ones. Where such rotation, or swidden, agriculture can become problematic is when the forest cover itself is reduced, putting pressure on agriculturalists to return to fallow lands earlier than their traditions would customarily mandate.

For many, however, both kinds of agro-forestry are to be vilified. Entirely misunderstanding the process, they see them as primitive and backward rather than the complex evolutions of use they generally are. Thus, the tragedy of missed opportunities abounds in Dowie's many cases. While conservationists and displaced communities share a common goal — the protection of as much of the natural habitat as possible — the people who might have provided crucial monitoring and protection because it was in their interest to do so have been and continue to be pushed out.

The link between rights and resource protection is not new, however, nor confined to Indonesia. One early example came from the rubber tappers of Acre, in the Brazilian Amazon. In the face of evictions and deforestation perpetrated by cattle ranchers, Chico Mendes spent a lifetime defending the rights of rubber tappers and indigenous peoples. Much like Asian forest dwellers, they earned their livelihoods from sustainably harvesting forest products and cultivating a range of food items in forest gardens. Here too, the organization Mendes helped build began, and saw itself, as a peasants' union, the Sindicato de Trabalhadores Rural, or Rural Workers Union. It was affiliated at the time with the most progressive and combative trade union federation in Brazil, the Central Unica dos Trabalhadores, and Mendes considered himself a socialist. But the rubber tappers brought a fundamental proposal to forest conservation in 1985 with their campaign to have the government set up extractive reserves throughout the Amazon. It barred ranchers from the forest, protecting poor people who gathered rubber, Brazil nuts and other produce, and allied them to indigenous groups in the area as well as ecologists. This dual vision thus served to bridge a gap between politics and ecology, between rural and forest peoples in the Amazon and the traditional conservation supporters who tended to see the ecologically rich jungle as a sphere ideally closed off from any human activity. "In this way," wrote Franklin Rothman and Pamela Oliver in a study of the anti-dam movement in southern Brazil, "the rubber tappers were able to forge an alliance of their rural peasant-based struggle with urban segments of civil society, broadening the social and political base of the movement."

Both natural resources and forest or river dwellers are also affected by the huge hydroelectric dam projects many developing countries are building with the aid of World Bank loans. These projects have almost always been embarked upon in order to provide a cheap source of energy to industries, such as smelting or pulp-and-paper manufacture. So aside from saddling the populations of poor countries with debt, the World Bank aggravates poverty as millions of affected people lose their homes and incomes with next to no compensation. As a result, movements of peoples affected by dams have sprung up throughout the developing world.

In Brazil, dam projects have inundated and destroyed thousands of hectares of land and delivered thousands of communities of people just getting by into abject poverty. In 1979, the decision by a regional state electric company, Eletrosul, to dam stretches of the Uruguai River led to the formation of what is now known as the Movement of People Affected by Dams, or MAB. Learning from the experiences of the power company's earlier victims in other parts of Brazil, this new social movement found support early on from trade unionists, the Catholic Church and the National Council of Rubber Tappers Mendes helped establish before his assassination in 1988.

At first this social movement organized local communities, held meetings and pressed for what they considered fair compensation. But as Eletrosul proved intransigent, it gradually took on a more combative stance and sought to stop the dam building altogether. It gathered a million signatures on a petition to stop the project. When that had no effect, it began to kidnap site engineers, destroy markers and tamper with earth-moving equipment. At the same time, according to Rothman and Oliver, the framing of the anti-dam movement also shifted. "Initially understood as being a land struggle, as being 'about' peasants' rights to land and livelihood, (it) evolved into an environmental and land struggle, as being 'about' the destruction of natural habitat through misguided industrialization and agricultural policies."

Today, the MAB is able to mobilize tens of thousands of people and has stopped the construction of several dams, including those on the Uruguai. Although as Glenn Switkes of Berkeley, Ca.–based International Rivers put it, "given the authoritarian nature of Brazilian energy planning, projects never die, and they may always be revived to meet the economic or political interests of Brazil's power elite."

Thailand in the mid-1990s also strove to initiate an era of modernization and industrialization, creating thousands of new pockets of poverty along with the ensuing corporate and para-state profits. In reaction to these policies, communities of river dwellers who lost everything to the construction of the Pak Mun dam organized and developed what is today the Assembly of the Poor. The movement grew to unite many communities adversely affected by divergent elements of the Thai government's economic dreams. It includes landless rural workers, slum dwellers and forest peasants who, like those of Indonesia, have been forced out of areas they had long occupied when the government retroactively designated their land as forest reserves. Some five million Thai are forest dwellers; mistaken efforts to expand tree cover have created the contradiction wherein they are pushed out so that pulp-and-paper companies can plant eucalyptus.

While consecutive administrations have agreed to open dams on various rivers, only to rescind their promises and close them again, forest dwellers in the province of Mae Hong Son exemplify the collaboration Dowie suggests should be commonplace. Subject to eviction and imprisonment over the years, their traditional rotational farming system maligned by forestry officials, they decided to counter the image evoked by traditional conservationists. Encouraged by their local administrator, Pa-korn Kangwanpong, they decided to use GPS technology to make a land-use database of their area. Town hall meetings were held throughout the process, so that everyone agreed on the map data. Participants also suggested and voted on regulations to enhance forest protection based on the GPS findings. This information was brought to state forestry authorities, together with the argument that not only were the peasants taking good care of the park, but they were essential to guarding it against illegal burning and logging. Their innovations were persuasive: this participatory conservation model is being expanded to other districts in the province.

So the events at Rimpak were plainly occurring in the midst of a global collision between new ways of looking at natural resource conservation and traditional thinking. However, the conflict with Perhutani illuminates another equally, if not more, pernicious practice. Protecting forests and their natural resources from encroachment by the people who have always lived among them is a screen in many countries aside from Indonesia for allowing mining, logging, energy production and monoculture agro-forestry instead. In fact, many international conservation organizations work closely with what Dowie calls some of the world's most aggressive global resource prospectors. "Their argument," he added, "is that bringing these people on board, admittedly allowing them to greenwash themselves, allows some input into the way they do their business, the way they extract their resources. It's an endless debate, but one I think they are losing."

Perhutani itself is an example of the blurring between natural resource protection and exploitation taking place in nations where governments are rarely accountable to the society they are supposed to serve. More than half of company profits go to the government budget, millions of dollars derived from a monopoly on the marketing of teak as well as its domination of pine-resin production and trade.

Set up in 1961 by the post-colonial Sukarno government, its policies have essentially been a continuation of those of Indonesia's Dutch colonizers. Ever since the seventeenth century, they considered the rain forest the property of the colonial state rather than of Indonesians themselves. Along with the famous spices for which the archipelago was once named, teak and other jungle tree species became a source of great wealth for them. Under the Dienst van der Boschwezen, native Indonesians were required initially to provide the Dutch East India Company with compulsory labour by logging the forests and later, to do this in lieu of paying land taxes. By 1873, as most of the native teak had disappeared into Holland's shipbuilding and furniture industries, a restoration scheme began. Known as *tumpang sari*, it permitted peasants to cultivate food crops among teak seedlings for a maximum of two to three years.

And much like Paulo Barros da Silva, who had no right to plant on his employer's unused land, in Indonesia under the Dutch, cutting down even one tree was a crime. It could earn the guilty the same kinds of steep fines and imprisonment Perhutani imposes today. Another similarity: villagers producing honey from the bees in Perhutani's forests are legally obliged to sell it to the company at a fixed, pre-determined price.

With control over 2.5 million hectares in Java alone — about 20 percent of the island's total — Perhutani has caused mayhem in a multitude of forest communities. In Cibaliung, for example, in 1998, the company evicted 1500 families from land their ancestors had cultivated for generations, replanting all 3000 hectares of it with teak.

The journey to Cibaliung by motorbike from the SPI office in Pandeglang took several hours, a winding passage through staggered fields of paddy rice, undulating in verdant waves towards the vague blue outline of mountains in the distance. Along the palm-dotted Java coastline, tall narrow houses with tiny holes instead of windows lodged the wild swallows whose nests were collected and sold to China for soup. Village mosques raised bulbous metal domes over the treetops at regular intervals along our lengthy, mostly pastoral route, and mats of cloves left to dry on the pavement enveloped us in brief tunnels of scent.

Like Wonosobo, it was difficult to picture privation in the midst of such beautiful surroundings. Yet in this, the most populous island of Indonesia's more than 17,000, they could only mask the repression of the recent past, the hardships of today and the continuous outward flow of families from its covert poverty to the more blatant version in the big city. "Most villagers have absolutely no idea about how to solve the problems they have in this harsh life," said Nova Trisnandar, better known as Oyo, the twenty-seven-year-old communications coordinator for Banten province. "People always think that the root of their problem is money. We have to grow it in their minds that the main problem is not about money but other things. But it's rather hard," he admitted. "You cannot do it quickly. Maybe it will take several years."

By the time we arrived in Cibaliung, the paved road was long gone, replaced by rutted narrow lanes, and the brick cottages with their peaked, tile roofs by structures of bamboo and thatch. We stopped at the home of a couple named Sanubani and Harpi, a large, airy but run-down house with walls of *bilik*, or woven bamboo. Jute sacking over the doorways rippled languorously in the stifling breeze. "Please forgive my humble house," said Harpi, arranging the few mats on the floor. Instead of tea, we were offered palm sugar in hot water to drink, as Oyo went out to purchase a few bags of salted snacks.

Sitting knees up on the floor, leaning his back against one wall, was an older man in worn black trousers and a navy-blue windbreaker. This was Marda, president of the SPI in Banten. "Since the era of our ancestors," he began, "we have used the forest here to plant rice. We plant in one place and keep another fallow. Then, after a while, we move to the other part, so that former land will become a forest again. It's like a pattern, one that we have used for centuries."

But when Perhutani took their land, he said, "the peasants could do nothing, because Perhutani was being helped by the government. There were many policemen with guns and other weapons, backed by local gangsters."

"It was like a war," said Yusuf, a small, wiry man of thirty-seven, with dark curly hair and a determined gaze. "A war against the people, against the peasant." He arrived wearing a tee shirt with the words "Penjara Tidak Membuat Kami Jera" on it, which means "Even Though We have Been in Prison We Will Struggle."

Before their forest farm plots were taken from them, the average family income in the village was the equivalent of about $800 a year — enough to live well and educate their children, Marda reckoned. Afterward, the men of the village had nothing to turn to but journeyman farm labour, when they could find it, that only paid about $1 per day. For him, one of the worst impacts of losing their land was the resulting inability of the peasant farmers to afford to send their children to school.

In response, the villagers organized several protest demonstrations. "When Perhutani first took our land," said Marda, "we had a demonstration at the National Land Bureau and also at the House of Representatives in Jakarta. But after we did that, people from the government came and destroyed our houses. There were lots of incidents like that, lots of intimidation."

Taking the judicial route towards justice also proved futile. According to Marda and Oyo, maps showed that the land in Cibaliung was not in Perhutani's jurisdiction. Rather the company had included it as part of the Laja Goa nature reserve in another region of Banten called Cikeusik. "They moved the boundaries and enlarged that forest," said Marda. "Perhutani will gain a lot. There is more wood to be planted, more teak and more mahogany." The National Human Rights Commission gave them free legal aid, "but because we have no money, and Perhutani has lots of money, after a long legal process, we lost the case," he said. "The court said there had been no changes to the boundaries. So it was corruption."

Meanwhile, as part of the government campaign against them, at least fifty-seven men from Cibaliung have been arrested and given jail terms of a year or more, accused by Perhutani of destroying forest. One of them was Yusuf. He had joined the Banten Peasants' Union in 1995, after learning about it from a friend, the son of a prosperous local man who had gone to study at university. Shortly after the eviction, in the year 2000, the local police grabbed him one Friday morning when he was on his way to prayers. "So it was very inhuman," said Yusuf, "very inhuman. After I was captured, I was stripped and thrown into a police car and taken away."

Yusuf was accused of damaging a hundred hectares of forest and taking tons of timber, "something that was quite impossible for someone like me," he said. "The evidence was only a small machete that we use to clean weeds or chop bushes. It's irrational and certainly a lie, a very obvious lie. I believe I was imprisoned because I struggle for the rights of the people."

In spite of the spurious charge, Yusuf was given an eighteen-month jail term. This left his wife Khaeriyah and daughters Yuhani and Siti Zuleha in such dire circumstances that they had to go to the city of Bogor and live with Khaeriyah's parents for two years. Yusuf believed that the arrest was designed to make an example of him, "a warning to other peasants from Perhutani and the government. If you try to fight us, this is what will happen to you."

Nonetheless, more than 200 SPI members in Cibaliung and its five surrounding hamlets did fight back by occupying and returning to swidden agriculture on land well inside the forest. According to Sanubani, they walked for two to four hours a day to reach them, sleeping there overnight during planting and harvest times. Aside from cassava, soy beans, corn and peanuts, they took off a crop of dry rice once a year, then planted clove to be sold to the cigarette industry.

"Now we can harvest," said Yusuf, "even if we have to do it quietly, way inside the forest. At least we have something to live on. At least we can survive. I believe this is an improvement, a step toward our success in the future."

"Most likely," added Marda, " there will be more farmers going into the forest because of their needs." Such activism, he said, has proven to be the only way to improve their circumstances and find some measure of justice. "We don't believe in politicians anymore," he said. "We don't believe in political parties anymore. All they do is promise and do nothing in the end."

"It has been a very bitter struggle for me," Yusuf admitted, "but I will keep on struggling, and retain my spirit." When asked what gave him the strength for this after such devastating experiences, he answered simply. "My children."

Their participation in the SPI not only gave the forest peasants of Cibaliung encouragement to resort to such direct action but also brought them into contact with peasants in similar circumstances across Indonesia and from other countries as well. These meetings, said Marda, allowed them to share their experiences and learn from others. "At first," he added, "I thought it is only people in Indonesia who have this problem, but after I joined SPI, it seems as if almost all peasants in the whole world have the same problems. That means a lot to me. I feel support from many other people around me from so many different countries. We have this solidarity, so I have more spirit in this struggle."

Later that day, Oyo sketched out a long list of rural conflicts in Banten, from the 700 hectares of rice paddies near Serang that were to be converted into an airfield for the Indonesian Air Force, to ongoing conflicts with villages around Ujung Kulon National Park as it sought to expand its boundaries. "In Sobang and Cimanggu," he went on, "there are many conflicts between peasants and a palm oil company concerning more than 1400 hectares. And then there are lots of other smaller cases we haven't been able to handle because there are so many."

The son of rice farmers, Oyo had managed to attend high school in Pandeglang but had friends in Cibaliung. "There I hear about lots of problems faced by the peasants," he said, "lots of issues. By hearing about them, an awareness kind of started growing in my heart to help those peasants, not only with land ownership problems but other problems as well, like productivity. Then I thought that by joining the SPI, I could really help, not only in Cibaliung but throughout the country."

With 4000 SPI members throughout three municipalities in Banten, Oyo said much of his work revolved around education, as well as unifying and encouraging solidarity among people often accustomed to trying to solve problems on their own. The movement also made a point, he added, of seeking out peasant farmers in trouble, either with the government or corporations. After joining the SPI, he noted, "there is of course a significant change in the way they look at their lives and their problems, and basically it's because of education. Once we have several small victories, they begin to feel more optimistic, to know more about how to handle these problems."

Caught between conservation and the agro-forestry business, such dilemmas are proliferating for the inhabitants of Indonesia's forests. Under pressure from activists and academics alike, Perhutani has reached agreements with some forest dwellers, increasing access rights as well as the amount of territory included in social forestry programs. Indeed, so-called community-based forest management has, over the past few years, become a new buzz phrase for forest bureaucrats.

Essentially, however, it is just a new name for *tumpung sari*. Under such agreements, peasants may use land for short periods of time to cultivate food, in return for looking after monoculture crops of teak, mahogany or pine. While some communities have wrested more secure, long-term management rights, for many others there is no security of tenure, nowhere to plant once seedlings grow into trees and only a quarter share of the value once the timber is eventually sold. They also have no say over how many trees are planted or which species. Who really controls and monopolizes the bounty of the forest is the corporation, and, as Kito Haryanto put it, "the basic goal of a corporation is to make profit."

The Ministry of Forestry, moreover, shows no desire to redistribute or reclassify state forest land, even if it has long been shorn of its tree cover. Instead of arriving at a beneficial arrangement of locally managed food production and reforestation, such as that undertaken by IPE in southern Brazil, the Ministry and its corporations — certainly their top decision-makers — cannot let go of their control. Rather than search for ways to partner with forest dwellers, giving them the lead in resource management and protection while improving their economic wellbeing with technology, micro-credits and free education and health care, they perpetuate conflict and social upheaval. Thus, in Indonesia, community-based forest management is not all that its name suggests.

Would Perhutani have stood back from its confrontation with the forest peasants of Rimpak had they not organized and protested? The stories of innumerable others like them, of forest dwellers who remain invisible to the state, corporations and even some big international NGOs, would suggest not. Together with that of Rimpak, however, they provide a vision of social justice for the poor actually strengthening and broadening the global struggle to preserve our environment.

While still a nascent grouping within the SPI, the dominance of the forest sector in Indonesia means it will continue to grow, said its education coordinator Syahroni. "The SPI sees the forest as an area facing many problems," he said, "whether it is social, ecological and also the economical problems of the forest dwellers. In the context of our struggle, which is agrarian reform, the condition of the forest peasant is also part of the organizing focus."

As much as their achievements, that struggle, that determination to "organize every peasant who suffers from injustice," as Syahroni put it, illustrates how the disparate causes and contexts of poverty require solutions from below. And even as those solutions are born locally, their potential is clearly far wider, offering the world a vital new approach to saving its increasingly endangered natural spaces.

• 4 •

Agriculture Is Life and Custom

The sudden arrival of a faceless power that takes away your land and your livelihood: this was an experience Somairi knew only too well. Since the series of military coups and machinations that brought Suharto to power in 1965, the wholesale theft of land from the poor by both private and public corporations occurred regularly throughout Indonesia.

When he was a child, Somairi's family lost its land to the state electricity company for the building of a dam. It left them with too little land to do much more than grow vegetables for their own consumption, and any prospect for his education and that of his six siblings vanished. "Before the 1970s, the land had been used for generations by the peasants," he explained, sitting cross-legged on the hard wooden sofa in the Wonosobo office. "But then, suddenly, corporations started grabbing land because no one had any papers proving ownership."

The loss of their small acreages caused enormous suffering for many families, he recalled. "The custom here," said Somairi, "was to have large families, several children who could help work the land. 'Many children,' people used to say, 'bring many benefits.' But as their incomes disappeared, peasants could no longer feed themselves and their children. Several committed suicide. Some people stayed and others migrated to other areas. Some found jobs as carpenters or well diggers, but unemployment was a problem because most peasants only knew how to do one thing: work the land."

Suharto's policies marked a contrast with those of Sukarno, the man he overthrew. Sukarno had become president as Indonesia finally won independence from the Netherlands, and after a brutal three-year occupation by Japanese forces during World War II. While never a democrat — he had himself declared President for Life in 1963 — Sukarno did devise a constitution that espoused such ideals as free education for all Indonesians, agrarian reform and the use of public lands for the social good. His five principles, nationalism, internationalism, representative democracy, social justice and theism, were known as Pancasila and made up what Sukarno deemed a system of guided democracy. In a majority Muslim nation, with about 14 percent of the population professing other faiths, it also recognized freedom of religion.

However, these were the years of the Cold War; Sukarno not only came to depend on the support of the country's Communist Party, the PKI, but also helped found the Non-Aligned Movement. In doing so, he earned himself a reputation as a crypto-Communist and the unrelenting ire of the United States. When Suharto came to power by force, it was seen as a major enhancement of U.S. interests, one that never lost its burnish even as his army massacred at least half a million Communists, trade unionists and peasant activists. Another 1.5 million people were jailed, and independence bids in Aceh, Papua and East Timor suppressed at the cost of hundreds of thousands of lives. Nonetheless, this dictator was considered a staunch and valuable U.S. ally.

Suharto opened the archipelago nation to foreign economic interests, mostly from the United States but also from Europe and Japan. Laws on foreign investment were revamped, oil and mineral concessions granted to foreign investors and an authoritarian regime established that kept wages extremely low and workers unable to organize — or protest. Called the New Order, political and economic circumstances became what U.S. writer Dan La Botz has called "a return to the kind of colonial relationship that Indonesia had to the Dutch."

The redistribution of farmland that had taken place during the Sukarno years also came to a halt. The New Order rapidly reversed previous land policies, which for twenty years had seen the Indonesian government move to reclaim land controlled by Dutch and other foreign firms and distribute some of it to farmers. While he left the Basic Agrarian Law intact, Suharto found other ways to counter it. According to Andrew Rosser, at the University of Adelaide, "As part of attempts to attract mobile capital back into the country by creating better conditions for investment, the New Order introduced several changes to land policy including downgrading the Ministry of Agrarian Affairs to a directorate-general in the Home Affairs Ministry in 1967, introducing a new law that abolished land reform courts in 1967, and discontinuing the annual budget allocation for the land reform program in 1971."

As investors sought more and more land for commercial use, Suharto also introduced so-called release-of-title procedures. As Rosser described it, these "created a mechanism by which enterprises could acquire titles to land without breaching" the Basic Agrarian law and its prohibitions on corporations owning land. "Upon release of the title," he wrote, "the land would become state land, allowing the state to award rights of use, building or exploitation over it to enterprises or other parties depending on the type of investment project."

Such a procedure also informed the new forestry law, introduced in 1967 and described in Chapter Three. By determining forested, fallow and peat lands to be property of the state, the government was able to hand out lucrative concessions to entrepreneurs and investors. It didn't matter if other people were already living on or using that land. This allowed, for example, open mining in areas not only of productive forest but also in protected and conservation forests. Land belonging to the Karonsi'e Dongi people was awarded to then-Canadian-owned Inco on the island of Sulawesi in 1975 and became the site of the world's largest open pit nickel mine. Placer Dome, which is owned by Barrick, is exploiting gold deposits in the jungle-clad Meratus Range in South Kalimantan. Both the indigenous Dayak and even local government have come out strongly against the project in an area of tropical forest that has been protected since 1928.

What's more, Suharto suppressed freedom of speech, assembly and the right to organize. Grassroots organizing and protest were not only forbidden but punishable by lengthy jail terms. The only peasant union allowed, the Farmers' Solidarity Union, was made up of military and big landowners and affiliated to Suharto's party, Gulkar. Army posts occupied every village, as local governance ceased to promote the interests of villagers and became instead a tool to mobilize and control them for the state. And if the country's GDP grew by an annual average of 7 percent over most of the three decades of Suharto's grip on power, many of those economic gains melted away during the Asian Economic Crisis of 1997–98. By then, Suharto and his family had engorged themselves at the trough of national resources: Transparency International puts the amount as high as $35 billion, making him the world leader with the worst case of kleptocracy in history.

As tea, palm oil and rubber plantations swallowed up areas where they had previously cultivated rice and other food crops, peasant families were prohibited from setting the terms of compensation, seeking justice or even complaining. Doing so meant they were Communists, and thus, faced with eviction, said Somairi, "people had no choice." The police and army were on the side of both state and private corporations and had no qualms about intimidating people, beating them and burning down houses in order to make them accept their fate.

Yet so much corruption and injustice and so many glaring disparities between rich and poor also fostered a sense of rebellion within many. For people like Somairi, resistance lay always just beneath the surface. "Yes, I care a lot about the struggle," he said, "and it is related to my experiences. I have lived a bitter life because of the violation of my family's rights. Once I knew the whole history, I really wanted to help those who share the same problem. Maybe that is why I have this strong sense of commitment."

Somairi had been involved in the struggle for peasants' rights in his region for almost a decade. His title, president of the Central Java Province SPI, may sound important, but he received no salary for it and was busy all the time. With only 600 square metres of land to cultivate, Somairi's wife supported the family of four with a small shop selling household items in Maron, the village twelve kilometres from the city of Wonosobo, where he was born. Sometimes, said Somairi half ruefully, his children asked him what he actually did for a living "and I never really know how to answer."

Despite the repressive state and its extensive apparatus, by the late 1980s, university students across Indonesia had begun to form small groups, discussing "what we should do in this rotten country," as Mohammed Ikhwan, the SPI's foreign affairs director, put it, "what we could do ourselves." Among them was Muhammed Haris Putra, then a student of communications in the Faculty of Social and Political Sciences at the University of Medan in North Sumatra province. Seated at a large table in a meeting room in the upper floor of the SPI's office, a two-storey house in a residential district of Jakarta, he clearly remembers how he became involved in what would eventually evolve into a national movement. It began with a campus study group, he said. "During this time, there were many study groups on the campus, and we had a critique of our courses, of all the contradictions."

Most of the students in this discussion group were the sons and daughters of peasants and workers, including Henry Saragih, now the SPI president, whose father was a plantation worker. Scholars of social movements have identified the advantage for organizations of the poor and oppressed in having a connection to an educated class that, as Haris described it, "has the same concerns." Franklin Rothman and Pamela Oliver pointed out the "blurring of boundaries" that can take place between external institutions and the mobilized poor, "when the regional priests and university professors are adult children of peasants in the area. Case studies repeatedly find that people with dual or complex identities are important 'network bridges,'" they wrote, "between political communities who aid the flow of information and resources between them. The Gramscian 'organic intellectual' remains an important feature of many local mobilizations."

According to Haris, his group decided in 1989 that it should look for ways to help peasant communities and chose a village of about 250 households called Lobu Ropa. One member of the group was studying micro-hydro projects, and in Lobu Ropa, Haris explained, "there is no electricity, but the electrical wires pass over it. When we first went to the village," he added, "we are not critical enough. It was like a charity, what we were doing; we wanted to help." However, neighbouring peasant villages soon got wind of what the students were doing and, identifying an opportunity, started travelling to Lobu Ropa to tell them about their problems as well. "They see that there are students there," said Haris, "very concerned with the people, with the peasants, and most of them who came to us had land conflicts, expropriations by plantations, mostly plantations."

The Medan students didn't have any kind of template to call upon so that the entire enterprise was a learn-as-you-go experiment. This may be one of the reasons it succeeded; it had no pre-conceived notions of what to do or not do. Rather, said Haris, they continually questioned and discussed what they were doing, including their vision of "bringing development" to the peasant village. The only intellectual influences the group did consider useful, he recalled, were the ideas of Brazilian educator Paulo Freire and alternative social science theories such as participatory research. For them, this meant not only talking to the peasants about all of their problems but also centring the quest for solutions on their activities and decision-making.

The students decided to try to bring some kind of structure to the conflicts in which they were becoming increasingly involved. "During that time," said Haris, "during the New Order, you can't have five people together. That will bring problems. The detentions, being put in jail, is a fact, a reality, and it happened to us." The only type of association the law allowed was the foundation. By then involved in sixty land disputes, the group called itself the Synthesis Foundation and called its peasant activists, researchers.

The members of Synthesis Foundation started to communicate with like-minded students organizing struggles in other parts of the country. At one point, they held a meeting and, in order to avoid detention, hired a boat to sail on Lake Toba as if they were tourists, cruising around it various times while they discussed strategies and shared experiences.

Their continuing analysis of what they were doing brought forth interesting conclusions. One concerned their role in the organization, recognizing the importance of the peasants themselves in managing the struggle, while not forgetting that they too were of the peasant class. Another discussion convinced them to spend time on the formation of cadre in a more systematic way. They also analyzed the potential repercussions of involving themselves in a struggle, even one with a successful outcome, then departing to engage in other struggles elsewhere. Haris compared this to being like fire fighters, chasing conflagrations. "What happens when the fire is put out?" he asked. "So we realized we needed to talk about a more conceptual movement. So it's not only when the conflict is very hot, also after that. We were thinking about when we start to organize, it is not only to reject the enemies," he explained, making a brushing movement with his hand, "but also to make a fair land distribution among the peasants, and also among men and women. The women also acted to reject (enemies), but afterward they still don't have land, so we talked about this." They even believed, as early as 1991, that what was needed was a national and autonomous organization of peasants united across the vast and varied regions of Indonesia's many islands.

Haris himself marvelled at the fact that until then, none of them had ever actually read the Basic Agrarian Law in the nation's founding constitution.

In those days, he said, "it wasn't possible to find it in a book or text. It was not like now with the internet." When they finally did, "we said to ourselves, 'Oh, this is what we have done.'" Meanwhile, of the sixty land conflicts in North Sumatra in which he and other students were involved, said Haris, "we won fifty-nine. We lost one because we came late and they had already gone to court."

In fact, peasant activists realized early on that taking the para-state entities or private plantations to court for land theft or evictions was not a solution. "Our analysis was that the law is the result of the political dynamic," said Haris, "so we cannot use this. We knew that there were so many cases where the peasants went to court and lost. And then they cannot re-enter an occupation because the court has already judged against them. In our opinion, going to court is very dangerous. So what we have instead is the day-to-day struggle, and the power of the masses. When the masses are strong, we can face these problems."

In 1994, still four years away from the end of the Suharto regime, the sixty local organizations in North Sumatra, each targeting different corporations, decided to coordinate their efforts under the banner of the North Sumatra Peasants Union.

Meanwhile, similar struggles were taking place in other parts of Indonesia, in West Java, Banten, West Sumatra and Lampung; with the support of local students, peasants were organizing and fighting back, starting to re-occupy their former lands in spite of the repression. Small victories — 100 hectares here and 250 hectares there — were won in local areas. The issue of agrarian conflict was growing from a localized, regional one to a national one, as the members of these new, independent peasant groups started to do solidarity work and collaborate among themselves and with other movements throughout Indonesia.

Meeting with each other in a nation of islands extending over 3000 miles was, as Ikhwan put it, "very hard. It was very difficult to get to other regions because, geographically, it's impossible, and we had to travel by bus. And we have to deal with the police and the military." Nonetheless, he added, while essentially an underground movement, "between 1993 and 1997, it's the time for consolidating the movement, especially in Sumatra and Java. That is why they also make achievements in campaigns, in making networks with other movements and also with international movements. So they gain momentum."

In July 1998, three months after increasing public pressure and economic chaos finally brought Suharto down, nine peasant unions met in Lobu Ropa and formed the Federation of Unions of Indonesian Peasants, or FSPI. By then leader of the Sumatra Peasants' Union, Henry Saragih was elected president.

A year later, still unaware of the FSPI's existence, Somairi had grown sufficiently angry about the government's treatment of his village to do something about it. He and a few others set up SEPKUBA, the Peasants' Union of Kedu and Banyumas. As it grew, SEPKUBA began to demonstrate and demand negotiations with the electricity company, which won some peasant families the right to go back to the lands that had been expropriated and better compensation for others. Among the latter were the families of Somairi's village, Maron. They won a pledge from the company to give them one million rupiahs a year for infrastructure, although, he pointed out, they still needed to pressure them every year to pay up.

SEPKUBA then moved its "area of concern," he said, "to land ownership problems in the forest. And we also shifted our struggle to that of educating peasant farmers, to the importance of setting up cooperatives, political education and so on." Somairi described this process as one of "educating peasants about their rights, but also their obligations as citizens, to unite themselves and become leaders, even though they are just common people."

In 2001, SEPKUBA and two other unions came together under a new name, the Central Java Peasants' Union, electing Somairi as its president. That same year, he said, "we held a demonstration at our local legislature, and it was covered in the national press. Henry Saragih saw this and he invited us to a national training course on advocacy for peasants." By the following year, the Central Java Peasants' Union had joined FSPI, giving it, said Somairi, "the conditions to start to struggle on a national level."

The years following Suharto's ouster became known as Reformasi, or the Reform, and over this period new movements and political parties sprang up and operated with relative freedom. Yet regime change has not signified a substantial break in the government's development priorities. Successive parties elected to rule have by and large continued to direct material, political and financial advantages to domestic and international investors. Meaningful land reform remains thwarted, and the attempt in 1999 to amend the law to stop mining in forested areas received so much opposition from corporations and their political supporters that few projects have been effectively either closed down or prohibited from starting up. As Rosser pointed out, "poor and disadvantaged groups remained weak compared to the politico bureaucrats, the major domestic conglomerates, the (international financial institutions), Western governments and controllers of mobile capital."

Although permitted to organize and campaign openly, violence against peasant activists has continued, as have the hundreds of detentions for protests against agrarian injustice. In September 2005, police fired rubber bullets and teargas into a crowd of about a thousand in the village of Tanak Awu, near Lombok, in West Nusa Tenggara province. The protestors were demonstrating against a government plan to build an airport on their farmland, even though an already existing airport could be extended to bring in the jets full of tourists the government was hoping to accommodate. Along with wounding twenty-seven people, the police also beat several others and jailed four of them. Ten more were jailed the following November, as opposition to the expropriations of fertile farmland continued.

Meanwhile, in the North Sumatra villages of Sei Kopas and Simpang Kopas, five people, including a fifty-five-year-old woman activist, were arrested by local police and jailed as part of a lengthy conflict with the powerful Bakrie Group, a palm-oil producer that was attempting to recuperate hundreds of hectares of land the SPI has occupied since 2003. More recently, three members of the Damak Mahilo SPI in South Sumatra were put on trial for attempting to take back their land from the Adolina Garden plantation.

Arrests of activists have also continued in Banten, with two SPI members arrested in 2007 for allegedly damaging the Ujung Kulon National Park. And on my trip back to Jakarta from Wonosobo, I stopped in Batang, where days earlier police had destroyed acres of food crops in the village of Kincono Rejo. Just as he was preparing to harvest, forty-eight-year-old Soeroso saw his half-hectare plot sprayed with defoliants and the protective trees surrounding it chopped down. The crops of fifteen other peasants suffered a similar fate. They had occupied land that had been the subject of a national certification project funded by the World Bank in 1993. Instead of going to peasant farmers, however, ownership titles had been given to political cronies of the village headman. "We have always used that land and the peasants believe that the land belongs to us," said Soeroso. "Every night I pray that the situation will get better," he added, "but I will also demonstrate at the local legislature, and replant my land."

About a week after that journey, I woke up in the house of Antos Met, in the hamlet of Sibaladuang on the island of Sumatra. It was a modest, not to say poor, house of plastered brick. Although solid, an air of privation seemed to take over the further in one went. From the living room with its heavy, upholstered furniture and dusty pictograph of "Allah" made from sequin-dotted cotton balls, to the rudimentary cement kitchen, it progressed to an even more minimal back kitchen, the toilet and well outside, where a battered black plastic pail dangled over an unwieldy lid of corrugated metal. In fact, this house belonged to Antos's mother, Rusnati, for here, society is both Muslim and matrilineal. Antos, twenty-nine, head of the local SPI base, no longer lived in his mother's house. Rather, it was his brother-in-law Adrianis who worked the family's half hectare of land, while Antos farmed a hectare of paddy rice and another quarter hectare of vegetables, all divided into four separate plots belonging to his mother-in-law.

While both households earned extra money from other jobs, tailoring in the case of Antos's sister Reni, and carpentry in his own, their cultural identity was deeply instilled in peasant life. "Agriculture is life and custom," he said. "Since Indonesia is an agricultural country, I hope that the government will care about smallholding peasants, about making life better for the peasant, but no, the government doesn't care about the peasant."

As daylight began to flood the house's main rooms, a breakfast of banana fritters, sago gelatin and hot tea was set out on orange-and-yellow woven plastic mats. Soon afterward, an elderly man in green trousers, blue polo shirt and Converse running shoes dropped by. Datuat Patia, sixty-eight, was a local clan chief, a position passed on, according to Minangkabau tradition, from uncle to nephew. He and Antos talked about how the village SPI base came together, when its inhabitants all decided to reclaim 66 hectares of their collective land in 1998.

The land had been taken from them by a rancher, who already owned 80 hectares and was politically well connected. But as the political situation changed and the villagers of Sibaladuang organized themselves in the SPI, they realized the time was right to take it back, in some ways as much for their honour as economic considerations.

Five hundred people, including children, said Antos, occupied and set up a camp on the land. "A smaller group went to demonstrate in front of the parliament" in the provincial capital of Padang "and ask to have the land given back to the peasants," he said. Alerted by the rancher, police showed up and told the peasants to leave, "but we outnumbered them," said Antos, "and so they didn't succeed." The rancher and police pressured the people for seven days before finally giving up. "We could only do this after Suharto left," Antos added. And according to clan chief Datuat, smiling broadly as he recalled that time, it was he who tore down the ranch sign over the driveway. Now this land was being farmed organically and had become an example of the ecological, chemical-free future the SPI had begun to envision for the rest of its members.

At its centre lay the new organic farming school in nearby Nagari village, a showpiece of learning and experimentation on two hectares of gardens, fruit trees and rice paddies. I was taken there by Rustam Efendi, a member of the provincial committee, whose English, while eccentric and rather endearingly — if confusingly, at times — informal, would be my only path to communication with his Minangkabau-speaking comrades. A tall rangy fellow with a square jaw and jocular manner, Rustam was from West Pasaman, where he had participated in a lengthy and violent struggle to reclaim land taken by a palm-oil company, one that resulted in the death of one union member and the imprisonment of many others.

A taciturn man named Adek, who had taken a six-month course in

Medan back in 2002, ran the school. Adek was chosen for the position, said Rustam, "because he is interested and clever," adding with customary wryness, "more clever than most." Beyond the small house where Adek lived with his family, dozens of varieties of vegetables grew in furrowed strips, often surrounded by flowering plants useful for fertilizing or pest control. At the bottom of a slope, a stilted pen had been built for the school's herd of goats. The manure collected below it was added to the piles of organically rich compost, which contained everything from leaves to burnt rice husks. They were also making a liquid organic pesticide, said Rustam, "but we don't use it much. We focus on how to manage different species of insects in this area. Some are bad, some are friends. You always have to figure out the needs of the plant."

Since its inauguration in 2006, said Rustam, about a hundred people had come there for courses, staying in simple structures made of wood and *bilik* also used for classrooms. Most of the students were SPI cadre, coming one day a week for a year, but local peasant farmers had also begun turning up to ask for advice. "When we built the school, everyone laughed," said Rustam, "but then they started coming, one by one." The following month, even the government would be sending a group of sixty students for an intensive, six-day course. Meanwhile, its broad choice of organic vegetables and fruit were being packaged at the school and distributed for sale in towns and villages nearby.

At some distance away were the rice paddies. Set within a much larger area of terraced green fields, they comprised the foreground of a postcard view of mountain ranges, purple and misty on the horizon. Streams of trickling water veined the cultivated landscape, running through swards of rice in various stages of growth, from the brilliant, almost luminescent green of bunched young plants to rippling fields of ripe, pale-gold grain. The yield from using organic methods was almost vertiginous: peasants were harvesting seven tons of rice per hectare, compared to just four or five using chemical fertilizers and pesticides. If, as Rustam said, the SPI began discussing organic farming "to see about how to lose our dependence on commercial fertilizers and the big companies that sell them," their endeavours had been enormously successful.

As morning progressed in Sibaladuang, a small group set out for its organic plot, where most of Antos's twenty-five-member base were working. Taking a break, they talked about the reasons they had decided to adopt organic practices, and in spite of the higher yields they were getting, no one mentioned that as motivation. "I do it first of all so as not to be dependent on fertilizers and pesticides from factories," said a man named Jastil, "because the factory gives the peasant very little information about what it really contains and what the effects are." Another simply expressed confidence in this latest SPI campaign. "As an organization, it has the power to kick out the ranchers and bring us many solutions and alternatives," said Beni, secretary of the Sibaladuang base, "to improve agriculture and our livelihoods."

But the most faithful adherent, perhaps, of organic techniques was Sukardi Bendang, thirty-nine, an SPI leader from nearby Tanjuang Pati, where he farmed one hectare of his grandmother's land and raised a few cattle. "I first got information about organic farming from reading about it in newspapers and seeing things on television," he said. "Shortly after, in 2002, I joined SPI. I discussed this with them and decided to take a one-week intensive course in Medan from the same teacher Adek had. After growing the first plot of organic rice, I felt really good. I got a very good crop, about 200 kilos more than by doing conventional farming."

Sukardi had moved back to his childhood home from the similarly named village of Tanjuang Pauh, where his wife's clan had farmed. "In 1996," he explained, "the government moved us because they were building a dam there and gave us two hectares for planting, and another half hectare for a house, in another place. But this land was very steep and stony, no good at all for farming." An NGO had initially organized the peasants against the dam-building project, he said, but once their funds dried up, they left. This NGO, said Sukardi, "only took on one project, the dam, but the SPI struggles for long-term issues that can last a whole lifetime."

In Tanjuang Pati, Sukardi began to organize the peasants there "step by step," he said. "I have invited members to start growing organic. And I still campaign so that the landless can get land and for agrarian reform. Government politicians just campaign and say that 'yes, organic is very good for the peasant,' but these are just empty words. They give no support for it. They only support the peasants who are in favour of them; they're the ones who get loans, for example. If we want these loans, we have to really pressure for them."

Sukardi had been so successful with his organic production that, not only had he recently been invited to work with the local farm board — a sign of official backing he took with caution — but he had also purchased two more hectares of land. Nevertheless, his primary reason, he said, for promoting organic farming so strenuously was because "it is healthy for families who eat our produce."

Like the school in Nagari, the SPI branch in Batang, Central Java, had also set up an organic showpiece. Although due to increased mechanization, finding enough cattle manure was a challenge, the branch still hoped to convince local peasants, members and non-members alike, that if they tried organic farming they would save money on fertilizers, grow healthier crops and harvest better yields. With new schools opening in Bogor, West Java, and in Lobu Ropa, training in organic farming methods has become intertwined with the SPI's overall efforts in the education of their members.

According to Syahroni at the central office in Jakarta, these efforts were of two types, political and technical. The former included basic workshops for "anyone who wants to join SPI," he said, as well as courses for their cadre, divided into five levels. Technical training was meant, he said, "to teach people to access the practical needs of the peasants," depending on where they were, so to speak, in their struggle. "For example," he explained, "if they are facing a conflict, we organize a course on advocacy, on how to solve problems and negotiate with the government and with bureaucrats. For members who have already reclaimed the land and have a problem with productivity, we organize courses on organic farming, on how to manage seeds and on money management. Also for young peasants, how to improve their administration skills. They learn computers and about journalism. And the last one is education on economic management, how to make a micro-finance cooperative, or set up economic institutions that can earn money to run the organization."

Donations from SPI members accounted for about a third of their budget, said Ikhwan, the rest coming from international NGOs and institutions. While such financing is certainly key to the running of a large organization of the poor, contributions from the bases — anything from a chicken or a basket of coconuts, to the dedication of one's talent and time — act as an important underpinning of personal participation and solidarity.

In November 2007, the FSPI altered the terms of its membership units from unions to individuals and became simply the Peasants' Union of Indonesia. According to Ikhwan, representatives at their annual congress who voted for the change agreed that this would help overcome difficulties in coordination and improve the movement's effectiveness. "It's not the autonomy," he said. "Autonomy is good… but if we have an education (initiative) here for instance but we don't have initiatives in other unions, it's difficult to have the same capacity or views, the same frame on the issues."

"If one union makes a demonstration or mass action," added Susan Lusiana, another coordinator, "the voice is not really strong on the national level. So unified into the SPI, our voice is greater and stronger, the whole organization is stronger."

Between twenty-five and forty families can make up a base in the organization, five such bases a branch and five branches a district. "So in one district we have more people and this can give dynamics to the political context," said Ikhwan. Decision-making remains decentralized, with the primary focus of struggle placed on district or municipal governments. This structure to a certain extent also reflects the decentralization policies enacted by the government in 1999 to spread political and administrative powers. It helps create a balance between the limited — but potentially sympathetic

— power bases at district, municipal and provincial levels, and the ultimate power held by the government in Jakarta. This was apparent in Wonosobo, for example, where its *bupati*, or regent, a man named Koliq, was supportive of the rights of forest peasants. He actually wanted to see 95 percent of the municipality devoted to forestry, and organic farming promoted among the peasants in the production forests, but his powers to enact such progressive measures were nonetheless restricted.

Autonomy and decentralized decision-making also encouraged what Ikhwan called, "the finding alternatives thing. Because Indonesia is very rich in cultures, very diverse cultures, we want people to think about the local wisdom they have to overcome these situations." While in some cases it can take a long time to make decisions, he added, "it's very rich in terms of the exchanging of experiences and different approaches."

The movement does, however, lay claim to a comprehensive ideological frame, one that is based on the principles of Pancasila and that they consider, in essence, anti-capitalist. "The main idea (of the SPI)," said Ikhwan, "is social justice, the right to land, fair prices, education and so on." To that end, they find political backing, not in any particular political party, he said, "but in the constitution, that means power to the people. We trace back the history and keep telling that to people, that the principles of this country are very anti-capitalist."

This assumption coincides with the experiences of Indonesia's peasant farmers, forest peasants, plantation workers and landless. If the idea behind Pancasila is that the resources of the nation ought to be enjoyed by the people, not its tiny corporatist class, it also makes sense when the SPI argues that international capital, in the guise of multinational agribusiness and global trade regulations, is not only harmful but unjust.

An extension of the push for land reform in Indonesia, the SPI's campaigning on a number of global issues is largely carried out through its participation in La Vía Campesina, which it joined in the early 1990s. Currently in Mozambique, until the end of 2008 its headquarters were based in the SPI office in Jakarta, with Saragih as its president. Some have criticized the SPI for determining its national agenda on international campaign priorities to the detriment of its national membership. Nonetheless, its campaign against First World agricultural subsidies and food dumping is one example of an issue that did have a great impact on local, smallholding rice growers and other producers. Intimately tied to the realities of even the poorest and least experienced of SPI members, it argued that such practices made small-scale family farming untenable and exacerbated migration to urban slums. In 2004, the SPI succeeded in persuading the government to ban cheap rice imports and donations.

However, in December of that year, when a tsunami destroyed much of

Aceh province, foreign donors rushed to send in food aid. The SPI complained that the country — and even Aceh itself — had plenty of domestic food supplies, especially rice. These, said Ikhwan, "were easier to deliver, more ecological and made more sense than importing food aid, which isn't even necessarily healthy food." In a coalition with other indigenous social movements, the SPI organized a community-based food aid and reconstruction process in Aceh, managed by local people and those affected by the tsunami rather than foreign experts.

More recently, the SPI joined with 184 other environmental and rights-based organizations to demand an end to large-scale and unsustainable palm-oil production in Southeast Asia. Destroying thousands of hectares of forest and peatland a year, Indonesia is the world's largest producer of palm oil, an industry that by 2008 was earning it $15 billion annually. As the mania for bio-fuels grows apace, the scale of environmental destruction and evictions of rural and forest communities only promises to worsen. One company in conflict with the SPI in Sumatra, for instance, Waringin Agro Jaya, is a member of the so-called Roundtable on Sustainable Palm Oil, an organization of corporations that claims to "promote the growth and use of sustainable palm oil." Thus, the connection between the family hectare of land, and landlessness itself, to government policymaking and the boardrooms of big corporations is as clear in Indonesia as it is throughout the underdeveloped world.

Members of the SPI have won or reclaimed a million hectares of land, a level of achievement made possible, said Ikhwan, "because the idea is concrete and the practice is also concrete. The idea is how to unite small producers, peasants and landless people to gain something, in terms of civil-political rights, as well as social, economic and cultural rights. The practice is raising awareness, building the capacities of our members and also more technical things, like workshops, technical training in agriculture and a new model, a new sustainable agriculture that we promote to the people. If the idea is not concrete and the practice not concrete," he said, "no one will understand." As an example of radical pragmatism, this neatly counters the prevailing belief system, one instilled since childhood in many poor nations and in Indonesia in particular, that there is "one view," that of the nation's ruling class. The aim of the SPI is to change that framework of stoical acceptance. As Ikhwan said, "If there are no struggles, the mindset is not changing."

Over the past decade, international institutions like the United Nations and even the World Bank have begun to emphasize the importance of self-organization among the poor. According to the Executive Summary of the U.N.'s Poverty Report 2000, "self-organization of the poor at the community level" is the foundation of poverty reduction. "Such self-organization," it reads, "is the best antidote to powerlessness, a central source of poverty."

As low-income nations become more democratic, it is thus believed that the poor and disadvantaged will be better able to build their organizational capacity, find new institutional channels open to them and contest the policies of their governments. Yet this view lets neo-liberal economic realities off the hook. As Rosser pointed out, "there is much more to empowering the poor and disadvantaged than simply improving their organizational capacity and changing the nature of political institutions." Indeed, the material resources of the forces lined up against the poor of the Global South are massively skewed. International investors and lenders, big conservation NGOs and Western governments — including that of Canada, which in March 2009 sponsored a mission of at least seven Canadian mining companies with the aim of "fostering a better understanding of geological opportunities in Indonesia" — still wield overwhelming financial power and influence. "Increasing the material resources at the disposal of the poor and disadvantaged in Indonesia," Rosser wrote, "would require a fundamental reordering of the global political economy and Indonesia's political economy in particular, neither of which appears to be on the cards."

The strength of grassroots social movements like the SPI and the Landless Rural Workers Movement in Brazil, therefore, lies in the fact that they go beyond the building of organizational capacity. Through direct action and the physical taking of land, their members are challenging the definition of empowerment that obscures the material basis of power. In identifying and attacking its political and economic roots, they are demanding a "fundamental reordering" and bringing greater than ever significance to their methods to combat poverty. And this refusal to accept the prescriptions of the world's powerful will be seen yet again in India, through the millions of urban slum dwellers who make up the Indian Alliance.

Throughout Indonesia, the system sows resistance to itself. Injustice and its converse, struggle, oblige an alternative understanding of reality and how to change it. And this explains why people like Somairi commits himself to organizing the forest peasants of Rimpak while living on nothing, and Yusuf to cultivating land to which he has no tenure, only the conviction of inalienable right. When an earthquake devastated West Sumatra in October 2009, destroying irrigation systems and homes — including his own — Rustam Efendi summed up the ethos of the Peasants' Union response in four words of his unique English: "peasants unity un breakable."

Part 3

India

· 5 ·

Beyond the Slum

It is difficult not to be daunted by Dharavi: Mumbai's largest slum — indeed the largest slum in all of Asia — a lot of taxi drivers outside the train station at Mahim junction don't even want to go there. Finally one agrees, negotiating the narrow streets around the station, then onto a highway crossing the noisome mangrove swamp lining the Mithi River, its name, which means sweet, an insult to its blackened state.

When he was a boy, Santosh Sabat could see Mahim station from the shanty house he lived in, and there was open space all around. Now thirty-seven, he can still remember how people had to put down stones or lengths of lumber to cross the many streams and marshes. Originally, this was a village of Kolis, or fisher folk, living along the banks of the Mahim Creek. But two centuries of migration and forced relocation have slowly filled in the swampy land and carpeted its 175 hectares with a map of contiguous settlements, called *nagars*. By 2007, about 600,000 people were working and living here in crowded, subhuman conditions. And as the entire metropolis of Mumbai expanded ever further north, a district once on the city outskirts now lay in its heart.

Migrants from all over the country had come to settle in Dharavi, so that it had become, in the words of author Kalpana Sharma, "an amazing mosaic of villages and townships from all over India." These ever-shifting waves of new occupants packed its warren of narrow lanes with shacks, shops and small businesses, like the one installing cable television Santosh bought four years earlier when the textile mill he worked in shut down. Dharavi was also home to sixty-two *pongal* houses, where legions of young men paid a few rupees a month to sleep, a massive recycling industry — the city's largest, employing 5000 workers — leather works, potteries and the infernal little place I saw when my taxi dropped me off at T Junction. Its murky space was taken up with a huge mound of discarded shoes and sandals, where three women toiled in the suffocating heat, frantically rubbing and cleaning them for resale. In the dual attack of sun and desolation on this mean little alley, their ill-paid work — and the life that must call for this — seemed as bleak as any could possibly be.

If rural poverty might at times be overlaid with images of fertility, with quiet and space, its urban twin offered none of this. It appeared to be what it was, ugly and distressing — and throughout the developing world, on an exponential growth curve.

Yet Dharavi was neither static nor homogeneous, its residents and workers, busy as they were, thinking about more than just making ends meet. Past the ubiquitous heaps of construction debris on the highway and families cooking lunch on its sidewalk, four new white buildings towered near T Junction, behind a sign that read "Dharavi Vikas Samiti." The Vikas Samiti, or Development Committee, did not belong to any state or municipal authority, much as these had by now set their sights on profiting from Dharavi's suddenly strategic location next to one of Mumbai's most sought-after commercial and residential suburbs, the Bhandra-Kurla Complex. Rather, with 5500 families, it was just one member group of the National Slum Dwellers Federation. The NSDF itself forms part of the Indian Alliance, a social movement of some two million urban poor, its progress in improving the lives of slum dwellers throughout India as unprecedented as it is inspiring.

A youthful-looking man with an unruffled manner, dressed in a long-sleeved white shirt and light blue trousers, Santosh was sitting cross-legged on the floor in the office of one of the tall white buildings. Above and around him, families from the NSDF lived in new apartments built to reflect their own particular conditions and specifications. Aware of how water and electricity supplies were often cut off on a daily basis, for example, they had stairs instead of elevators and toilets outside the living quarters on each storey. The corridors were wider than usual, so tenants could socialize, and a shady green ground area had been included for children to play. These four-storey blocks had taken the Vikas Samiti many years to build; even with the grant funding and members' savings in place, even as the city recognized the project as a sound one, seventy-five different permits were needed just to begin construction.

Now Santosh too was waiting for such a home. He had joined the Federation in 1991, he said. "I saw the work being done by the NSDF and that's why I thought that by joining, our lives would improve. Since childhood," he added, "I have had an interest in social work, so that's how, when people were talking about NSDF, I wanted to know more about it." By now, Santosh was on the committee of his local group of 160 families, the KOD Society. At society meetings, he said, they discussed "how to develop Dharavi, and the Slum Rehabilitation Authority scheme that has been stopped now. How to again start with this scheme so we can benefit from this."

The SRA had long been promising to rehouse the slum dwellers of Dharavi, yet years had passed and Santosh and his family still lived in the house where he had grown up. Ensconced within its scrappy profusion of tiny huts and two-storey *chawls*, steamy workshops and open cement sewers, this house would have been impossible to find without a guide. Heading off of 60 Foot Road, one of only two streets in Dharavi, along a series of ever smaller, zigzag pathways, past more and more rows of huts with their drying laundry and upended bed frames, Santosh followed a circuitous yet, for him, familiar route. We were moving so quickly that the tremendous visual impact of the giant slum was reduced to a series of brief images: rusty, tattered edges of corrugated metal, smudged stucco walls, a stack of baskets and a coffee-coloured goat. Finally, around a hidden corner and down a dark, tight passageway, we suddenly stopped and stepped down into a small flag-stoned space with lime green walls, lit with a fluorescent light and filled with women and children.

Santosh's wife, Geetanjali, was preparing a colander full of okra for lunch; taken by surprise, her first reaction was to swallow a smile and shyly cover her face with a corner of her sari. But she wasted no time in turning on a large box fan and sending eleven-year-old Sagar, just back from school and still in his pale-blue uniform, out again for cold bottles of Coke. She insisted we sit on her only piece of furniture, a bunk that ran across one wall wedged beneath a staircase and a shelf loaded with electronics: a television, a sound system and small shrine lit with multicoloured fairy lights.

The fan seemed to take up an absurd amount of space, as did a big blue plastic barrel of water. With two tiny areas, each about the size of a phone booth, for cooking and for bathing, I could picture how Geetanjali's day would be one of continually manoeuvring herself around bulky objects, children and visitors. Extending an arm through the doorway, she could easily touch the wall of the neighbouring house.

The hut had a loft where Santosh's father had lived until he died, but the family did not sleep up there. Instead, friends of theirs had taken it over, another family of four, which meant that eight people were making do in these two cramped rooms.

Outside was a tap that worked for a couple hours a day, but the closest toilet block, while not far, was a municipal one, noxious, filthy and converged upon every morning by long lines of people needing to use its disintegrating facilities. While the NSDF had worked with several neighbourhoods in Dharavi to build and manage their own toilet blocks, Santosh's family was unlucky enough to live near one still run by the city.

However, Geetanjali considered this to be a good house, she said. Before her marriage to Santosh, arranged by their parents when she was seventeen, she had never even left her village in Orissa. "In the village there was more space," she acknowledged, "the rooms of our house there were larger, and it was not so congested." And she wished there was somewhere further away to leave garbage; as it was, people simply dumped their refuse in any available patch of open space, to rot and swell the stench of the sewers. But for Geetangali, none of this was as bad as the flooding brought by each year's monsoon. She pointed to her younger son, eight-year-old Samir. "Last year, the sewage water came in higher than his head," she said.

Outside again, Santosh assembled a few more members of the society, as if to show that within all this chaos and desperation and patience with the unliveable, there were threads of activity that would eventually get them out. The group filled and all but blocked the tiny junction. Some passers-by squeezed through, but others stopped to listen and nod their heads, one little girl, her eyes rimmed with kohl to keep her cool and ward off the evil eye, pushing through our legs to stare.

A man named Kumar reckoned that as many as eighteen politicians had come to visit Dharavi over the past few years, always promising solutions to the flooding, the toilets and the crammed and awful living conditions. "But they only come for the votes," he said. "They don't actually do anything. Whether it's the Bharatiya Janata Party in power, or the Congress Party, it makes no difference."

"Exactly," said Santosh. "The only way we'll achieve anything is when people are together and trust each other."

"And we do trust each other," Mr. Kumar asserted. "As an individual you can't do anything on your own, but as a group we can. We can go to the government, make a rally or go on strike. Because we are organized, we know they have to listen to us."

From the air, the topography of Mumbai's slums is unexpectedly, almost eerily, visible. The flat, corrugated roofs of shanties surround every tall building or clump of tall buildings throughout the rapidly growing city. It is as if millions of equally sized rectangles of brownish cardboard have been dropped into a stream, to flow and eddy around every taller structure, into any space at all.

Looking like a hand thrust into the Arabian Sea from an immense sleeve, Mumbai has a population of 14 million in its metropolitan area alone, resolutely refusing to grow outwards, merely further and further north. Originally founded on seven islands, the port christened Bom Bahia, or Good Bay, by the Portuguese in the seventeenth century has been a vibrant and dynamic city for most of its existence. It was once known as the Manchester of the East thanks to its hundreds of textile factories, like the one that had employed Santosh. Today it is the hub of India's banking and financial sectors, home to diamond traders and steel plants, the world's largest movie industry, offshore call centres and technology-based enterprises. Even in Dharavi, it is estimated that businesses turn over $665 million annually. Current predictions, moreover, suggest that in just a few years, Mumbai will have grown to become the second-largest city in the world.

Yet the majority of Mumbaikkars, about 60 percent, live in its slums or on its pavements; in total, they live wedged upon only about 8 percent of the city's total area. The slums are incubators for ever-budding informal economies, including plenty of illegal ones, even as an estimated 40 percent of the city's police have been living in them since the force stopped constructing employee housing. While millions of huts have been built by and in a sense "belong" to their residents, millions of others pay rent to live in such inadequate housing, often to denizens of the city's underworld, who are heavily involved in slum landlording.

Masses of working poor also congregate within the interstices of the more affluent areas of the city to service the better off, as drivers, maids, sweepers, launderers and presswallahs (who iron clothing). They sort through refuse for anything recyclable, sell fruit, vegetables and snacks from the sidewalk and engage in a host of other survival activities. Overall, slum dwellers supply the city's burgeoning economy with a vast pool of cheap labour. Moving goods with their own energy, travelling for hours to bring all kinds of food and consumer items to street corners and people's homes for a low price, their homelessness essentially subsidizes the cost.

Those who have a structure on the sidewalk or in a settlement seem much better off than the millions who essentially sleep out in the open. For Mumbai is a city in seemingly permanent process. Walking along its hectic thoroughfares or taking a motor rickshaw from one place to another, I would see hundreds of people along road-widening projects and on building sites, simply occupying whatever pile of dirt was not currently being utilized. Surrounded by small children and the odd pet dog, women could be seen fixing a meal over a fire or scrubbing clothes on a patch of cement. Contractors hire labourers, many of them women, to work for the equivalent of about $1 a day breaking stones, digging and carting away debris by hand, so that entire families simply move in and begin living on their worksite. Every night, vast numbers of them rest from their labours on the ground or on the pavement. Many have been run over and killed by errant drivers.

That so many people can live like this seems extraordinary in the twenty-first century, and yet their conditions are reflected as if from a dark mirror throughout Asia, Latin America and Africa. Today over a billion people — 85 percent of all city dwellers in the Third World — live in slums, along transportation lines and on garbage dumps or other marginal lands edging mushrooming cities. They live in unbelievable yet, for them, customary wretchedness, denied civil and legal status. Despite their vast numbers, they maintain only the most tenuous relationship with the state, which is itself in a process of either privatizing or simply abandoning its services and social obligations. While distressingly, even staggeringly, visible to anyone who cares to look, officially, they are invisible.

With an estimated 200,000 people a day leaving the countryside for cities that cannot accommodate them, the United Nations is predicting that a quarter of the world's population will live like this by the year 2030. They are, wrote Mike Davis in *Planet of Slums*, "the fastest growing and most unprecedented social class on earth."

In African countries like Ethiopia and Chad, for example, 99 percent of all urban dwellers live in slums; in Afghanistan, it is 98.5 percent. Of the half a million people who migrate every year to India's capital, Delhi, four-fifths of them end up in its slums. It is Mumbai, however, according to UN-HABITAT, that has the honour of being the global capital of slum dwelling, followed by Dhaka, Lagos, Cairo, Karachi, Kinshasa, São Paulo, Shanghai and Delhi. "Instead of cities of light soaring towards heaven," Davis wrote, "much of the 21st century urban world squats in squalor, surrounded by pollution, excrement and decay."

And yet almost everyone who lives in a shack or on the sidewalk in Mumbai is working and earning some income. The problem, of course, is the scantiness of those incomes. The Oakland Institute estimates that 80 percent of India's population of over a billion live on less than the equivalent of $2.50 a day, and for half of them, it is less than $1.25.

What's more, as long ago as 1976, India's parliament passed the Urban Land Ceiling Regulation Act, which authorized using surplus land in the hands of private owners or the state for the public good. But the Act has never translated into action, into the alleviation of what one local newspaper called "Mumbai's stifling housing crunch." When I commented to a friend on the incredibly glacial pace in which the municipality went about signing off on funding for rehousing the poor, she said, "the problem is that many civil servants are poor themselves and don't have good places to live. They don't like it that a slum dweller can get a flat for free."

Yet there is more to slum proliferation than bureaucratic laggardliness. Land has grown increasingly expensive in Mumbai, tenure rights insecure or non-existent and the social relations that prevent government from losing control over the housing process — and the poor — are strong and deeply political.

The story of the NSDF began when the residents of a slum called Janata Colony started to mobilize in the late 1960s against an eviction notice from the city government. At the time, more than 70,000 people lived in the Colony, having ballooned from the original 4000 families the city had resettled there from south Mumbai in 1947. But as that land got earmarked for housing and recreation space for the 3000 workers of the nearby Bhabha Atomic Research Centre, built in 1952 with nuclear technology from Canada, they were ordered to disperse and leave. Their huts, along with the community's schools, temples, shops and flourmills, would be demolished. With the municipality now challenging their right of tenure, it was the way such things had always been done — and often still is.

This time, however, something changed. The people of Janata Colony organized themselves, bringing court challenges and resisting eviction for several years. Together with leaders of other communities facing removal, they formed the Bombay Slum Dwellers Federation in 1969 and the National Slum Dwellers Federation five years later.

The movement that would eventually evolve from these organizations, the Indian Alliance, is by now made up of five interlocked organizations based in seventy towns and cities throughout India. Crucial to its growth was the Federation's joining forces in 1986 with the Society for the Promotion of Area Resource Centres, or SPARC, established by Sheela Patel and other like-minded social workers just two years earlier. It was a move that brought together an activist group and an NGO on equal footing, with similar ideas on how to solve problems of urban deprivation and to empower the poor.

SPARC had been working with mostly women pavement dwellers in the Byculla district of Mumbai; together with the NSDF, it founded Mahila Milan, a network of women's collectives in federated communities associated with the NSDF, organized street children into a group called Sadak Chaap, or Stamp of the Street, and in 1998, set up a non-profit building and construction company called Samudaya Nirman Sahayak. Within the NSDF itself, women began to assume more influential roles and now form about half of their community leaders.

Through their participation in the Indian Alliance, members have acquired government ration books and access to water; they've set up community-run police stations in Pune and Mumbai and built more than 500 clean public toilets also managed by the communities; they have acquired or constructed housing for some 70,000 families, often more cheaply and of better quality than standard government projects, because they have been designed by the poor themselves.

Just as importantly perhaps, the Alliance has turned commonly held notions on poverty alleviation and housing on their head. It gives a voice to the poor, not only as they articulate their need for housing and other basic services but how to make these projects work best for them. It embodies a vision of citizens who are not helpless children accepting whatever largesse the state — as it surely likes to see the provision of low-cost housing — imparts, but protagonists in their own quest for, and right to, a decent life. In their assertion of an empowering identity and dignity, the membership of the Indian Alliance has become a force to be reckoned with, in both national and international development politics.

In Mumbai, the federation is divided into five smaller, self-run federations, based on who owns the land where their members are living — the airport, the railway company, or the municipality — and with which government body it must negotiate. These groups take charge of promoting their own struggles and of how to involve more and more people in those struggles.

One aspect of the success of this social movement is rooted in the vision of two of its founders. Sheela Patel and Jockin Arputham don't see themselves as leaders so much as facilitators, or providers of both the physical and psychological spaces that open up to the poor ways to begin solving their problems. By psychological space, I mean a frame that acknowledges not only the rights of the slum dweller but also his or her responsibility and abilities in achieving change in their lives. "When people come and say they want to change," said Jockin, "I say, you want your life to improve? Then you decide, not me." He called this "forcing people" to make a decision. As members of the Indian Alliance, it is the poor themselves who must not only become able to make changes but see themselves as able to do so. "I take the knowledge and communicate it to them and say, with your ground reality, you have to make that change," he said.

By not trying to replicate the role of development experts, this movement is both more innovative than, and qualitatively different from, well-meaning foundations, international development institutions, rights-based community organizations, traditional micro-finance institutions and certainly multi-lateral banks. And it is probably the unusual riches-to-rags personal history of Jockin Arputham that places this movement right within the confines of slum life.

Whenever he is not travelling, Jockin is to be found most mornings in the Vikas Samiti office in Dharavi. Plain and sparsely furnished, a large grey metal cabinet dominates the room, Jockin's glass trophy from winning the Ramon Magsaysay Award in 2000 — sometimes called the Asian Nobel Prize — posed on its top. Taking up most of the wall behind, a blackboard lists in chalk the Vikas Samiti societies and their collective savings, as much as 300,000 rupees, or $15,000, which are temporarily stored in the grey locker. A small man with thinning hair and the look of a pixie, his feet so small he had to wear children's shoes at his wedding in 1974, Jockin takes one of the few white patio chairs and seats himself against the wall nearest its open door, ready for consultation.

Some dozen men and women, individually or in little groups, sit on the linoleum-covered floor, each in turn pulling sheafs of paper from plastic carrier bags — the briefcase of the poor — to flatten their creases and corners. They explain circumstances, ask and answer questions. They listen intently as Jockin speaks in rapid-fire Hindi. They're all there "to find out about accommodation," one man whispers to me, inadvertently sounding a bit like a hotel desk clerk.

In 1963, when he was still called Joachim and Mumbai still called Bombay, Jockin left his home in Bangalore to, he says, "make my fortune." He was seventeen years old. At one time, his large family had been wealthy — "very orthodox, rich and feudal" is how he describes it. His father rose to become chief engineer at the one of India's largest privately owned gold mines, the Kolar Gold Fields, and owned a 40-hectare farm. "But we lost all our money because of my father's political ambitions," says Jockin. "When I was small, two servants accompanied me to school, one just to carry water for me, and by the time I was sixteen, I did not even have the water," he jokes. "So not unlike many migrants," he concludes, "I was struggling. I knew I was going to the slum. I went, and my life began there. You go to a city like Bombay and you have no other choice than to be a squatter."

When he first moved to Janata Colony, he recalls, all he could see were the shortages, "the shortage of water, the shortage of toilets, the shortage of everything. Everything was inadequate and that forced me to think about how this situation needed to be changed." Yet he did what so many slum dwellers do, picked up a trade — carpentry in his case — got married and started a family. And as Joachim became simplified and shortened to Jockin, he began involving himself in various community efforts, in setting up informal schools for children and getting water connections, collecting household waste and cleaning and whitewashing the public toilet. Throughout all these activities, he became aware of the abilities that slum dwellers in fact possessed to achieve such small, incremental units of improvement on their own. "I learned to do many things without money," he told David Satterthwaite of the London-based International Institute for Environment and Development, "to work with all this creativity among the inhabitants. Lots of things that needed to be done could be done without funding."

The creativity of the poor: often it is one of the few sharp-edged weapons in their arsenal of resistance. Overturning the tortured logic of bureaucracy, eluding the regulations put in place in order to put the poor in their place, it evokes in all of us the satisfaction to be derived from small victories over authority. According to Jockin, when the people of Janata Colony wanted to do something like connect to a water main, they would send a letter to the relevant city department stating, "If you do not respond in 10 days we will assume that we have your approval." Once, when the city workers who never came to make a legal water connection arrived to disconnect an illegal one, they surrounded it with hundreds of small children, all loudly reciting the ABCs from their schoolbooks. The simple but ingenious insertion of a railway ticket into the receiver of a public phone gave them endless free calls to government ministers in Delhi. And to get around State of Emergency restrictions on disseminating political material, they would deposit a kilo of wet handbills on top of ambulances. As these wended their way throughout the city and the handbills dried in the sun, thousands would fly off into the streets.

Yet the threat of demolition continued to hover over them. "There were two basic reactions," Jockin says, "when I started talking about organizing: What are your political ambitions? And, will it be sustainable?"

While Jockin had no such ambitions and, in spite of international recognition of his work, still doesn't, the government considered him a troublemaker nonetheless. In spite of his many devious ways of hiding himself, he was put in jail, by his own count, sixty-seven times. The situation grew worse when the State of Emergency declared by Prime Minister Indira Ghandi suspended all civil rights in June 1975. Eventually, in May 1976, just before the opening volley of that year's monsoon, Janata Colony was demolished.

However, the struggle for tenure rights the community had brought to the courts and to the streets did ensure it an alternative piece of land rather than wholesale dispersal. Ten thousand families moved to an area four kilometres further east called Cheetah Camp, where Jockin still lives. And there they started over, embarking on that same process of self-support — constructing huts, wiring electrical cables, getting water connections and setting up schools. Rather than succumbing to the power of authorities, they learned how to resist and manipulate it.

The resistance to the eviction of Janata Colony and the broadening organization underlying it also brought the issue of homelessness — which is what slum dwelling really is — nationwide attention. Over the decade following the founding of the NSDF, the movement slowly began to expand. Its strategies also evolved, from confrontation to a determination to convince government bodies that the poor are competent and responsible, that they own the expertise required for solving the whole housing dilemma. As Jockin put it in an interview with a Philippine journalist, "It was during these years that I saw a need to change the approach. I was doing all agitation, breaking this and that, being completely militant, but the material benefit to the people was zero."

This modification in NSDF strategy was a conscious one, underscored in its union with SPARC. Jockin's activism first brought him to Sheela Patel's attention while she was still a student at the Tata Institute of Social Work. Years later, she said, when she worked at Nagpada Neighbourhood House, "he would come to seek my advice on various funding strategies. In 1985, when we did the pavement dwellers study, he came to see what we were doing, and in 1986, he suggested that NSDF and SPARC work together."

In its combination of militancy and concrete achievement, the methods of the Indian Alliance bear some similarities to those of the Landless Rural Workers Movement of Brazil. Identifying and occupying places where they might build homes being pretty much what slum dwelling is already, it doesn't, however, challenge capitalist notions of private property by taking land. While it does consider secure and decent housing a right, its philosophy is more complex than simply agitating for its implementation.

When slum dwellers asked Jockin, "will it be sustainable?" they were thinking beyond how to find a better place to live, much as this might be a huge and important personal aspiration. As Jockin puts it: "You are going for something tangible, but the fallback is non tangible. Every aspect of a struggle has to have a long-term implication. It has a political objective, political change. And it has to have individual value change. The basis of the struggle is value change."

While value change may be difficult to comprehend in the context of dire poverty, it is one of the guiding principles that have made the NSDF and the whole Indian Alliance a successful grassroots social movement. It implies recognizing your own value and that of your neighbours, of the people who might work for you in your slum business, of different religions and of new-comers who take up more and more of your community's already limited physical space. "The poor need to understand that idea of value change," Jockin emphasizes. "If you don't have value change, whatever change you do make has no meaning."

As paths of identity are transformed and extended, the walls of caste and religion are broken down by solidarity and organization. Value change emphasizes the obvious parallels that have always existed among the poor. The importance of this in an urban movement of marginalized and un-dervalued people in a country with so much intra-sectarian strife can't be exaggerated.

In 1992 and 1993, for example, Mumbai was torn apart by a surge of violence in the name of religion. It was fuelled by Shiv Sena, a conserva-tive religious party that has for many years controlled the government of Maharastra state. Like other such parties in modern history, the pro-Hindu Shiv Sena blames others — in this case, Muslims — rather than the exigen-cies of capitalism, for all of society's economic and social ills. Hundreds of Muslims were systematically identified and massacred by Hindus, their homes and shops burned. In retaliation, some Muslims, especially in the underworld of organized crime, set off ten powerful bombs all over the city. The death toll at the end of this sectarian turmoil was 1400 victims. Yet slum areas where the Alliance had organized were spared. "There was no violence in any of the Federation communities," said Jockin. "In fact Muslims came to the Hindus to relieve and console them, and vice versa. This was a most important thing in our Federation and I am very optimistic about it."

Experience has taught Jockin this much. Usually about 20 percent of poor people in any given community are, he says, "sitting on the fence; they will go with whoever is winning." Fifteen percent don't care and are only after what they can get, while a similar number are what he calls "the political analysts, who say 'this is not good enough.' But they can be good support. But the remaining 50 percent," he enthuses, "are the ones who keep the energy going, who are concerned about their neighbours, who believe in collective responsibility and push for collective decision-making. That's what keeps me going; that is my dream and what keeps this movement alive."

He points to the women at the far end of the office, huddled over the savings books at low-legged tables, close to the big grey locker. "They don't just put money in there," he says. "They put their hearts in there. You take money from a man, he shouts, he screams, he forgets. But the women, no. They are investing in the quality of life."

For Jockin, the whole movement lived on what he calls "the energy of the women's strength. They are the backbone of this movement," he says, "all through the Federation. So women mean to me, in other words, money, next, communication; women mean, very importantly, information."

The largest housing project to which members of the NSDF have moved by now, however, was somewhat different from that in Dharavi. It was located in Lallubhai, in the Mankhurd district of Mumbai, at an inconvenient distance from its train station on the Western Line. Still incomplete by 2007, Lallubhai Compound was an Eastern Bloc–style project of long, five-storey apartments built in two rows, constructed by the city with money from the World Bank. People living there have to take a long bus ride downtown or pay for a motor-rickshaw to reach the railway station. The project was not, as SPARC social worker Sharmila Ginonkhar said, "designed for the poor." Yet it was destined to become home to 10,000 slum families, half of them moved by road widening projects, the other half from the railway tracks and organized in the Alliance.

Mumbai's train system knits the entire metropolitan area together from north to south, not only for the poor but the working class in general; for the city's famous tiffin wallahs delivering meals, for students, office workers and street vendors heading to prime spots for their daily trade. To me, the station names — Cotton Green, Matunga Road, Mumbai Central — sounded like titles to a novel, yet the real drama concerned the tens of thousands people who lived in dense rows of shacks, at times as many as three deep, on the spare margins of land along either side of their tracks. Rushing into view through the metal-grilled windows of the train carriage came the huts and structures swathed in plastic sheeting, the people in them, their few possessions — including, once, a morose looking monkey — before disappearing again into oblivion.

Yet for those living in the railway slums, those anonymous figures glimpsed only for an instant, life was all but unendurable. While either huts or spaces to build them were bought and sold, finding water was a challenge met only by long trips on foot, rattling noise a daily constant, relieving oneself in some modicum of privacy only possible at night. At times, the crush of huts was so close to the trains a passenger could reach out and touch them. Every year, there were injuries and accidents, especially with small children, and trains were forced to slow down through these tunnels of misery, causing havoc with their schedules.

In 1996, Indian Railways decided to move the 60,000 families living in railway slums, eventually joining a complex group of bureaucracies under the aegis of the Mumbai Urban Transport Project, to do so. Through the 20,000-member Railway Slum Dwellers Federation and Mahila Milan, the Indian Alliance also became involved in the $175-million project. The process that began by counting as accurately as possible the number of households to be resettled, and ended with resettlement itself, took several years. At one point, in 2001, Indian Railways even defied the established procedure and began demolishing hundreds of shacks before there was alternative space available for their residents.

The MUTP process in many ways illustrates how the Indian Alliance functions and spreads among the poor. The moving of the railway slum dwellers to new homes began with a census, carried out by other slum dwellers, who understood better than any bureaucrat what slum life entailed. It was also an effective recruitment tool for the Alliance. In the railway slums where they had yet to organize, enumeration introduced people to the Federation. Not only was the impending move — and how the slum dwellers themselves wanted it to evolve — discussed, but also the importance of organization, of setting up savings circles and being prepared for new homes and a different life.

Most importantly, perhaps, it gave the poor control over knowledge about themselves and reversed the usual planning process. Rather than outside experts coming in and gathering information before presenting a proposal to communities that could do nothing more than disagree or acquiesce, the railway slum dwellers themselves actively engaged in preparing the census and generating solutions. For Arjun Appadurai, senior advisor for global initiatives at the New School in New York City, these strategies of self-enumeration and self-surveying "have created a revolutionary system that we may call governmentality from below, a crucial part of what I have called deep democracy."

As such, it was instrumental in assuring that the final count recognized the realities of these elongated communities, with neighbours explaining how many families lived in one hut, or who was not at home, or whether a family owned more than one structure. The Alliance also pressured the

MUTP to recognize the rights of later arrivals, moving the cut-off date up from 1980 to 1995.

In fact, these discussions with Alliance enumerators were the first inkling most of those living along the rail lines had that the city was planning to move them. For Madhuri Kisan Karat, a hermaphrodite, or *hijra*, rejected by her family at the age of fifteen, the visit from a census taker "was how we came to know that our houses would be demolished, and we would be shifted from the Harbour line."

Madhuri made her living by showing up at homes where a wedding was taking place, or a new baby had been born, to bestow the auspicious blessing these differently gendered people are believed to be able to confer. She had purchased a small plot beside the railway track near Andheri station for 1500 rupees in 1987. There she paid 400 rupees a month for use of a water tap half a mile away and could go to the toilet only between 8 p.m. and 7 a.m., when a particular train was left for the night on a siding.

Madhuri described her slum as "a filthy place, where there were many illegal activities going on. There were people who were drinking and doing many wrong things. So people were fed up with all of these things. They were saying, 'it's better that there is some organization,' because none of the political parties was taking care of us."

Another railway slum dweller and area leader, Abdul Karim, could re-member the exact day he joined the Federation — February 1, 2001. With his only son working in a tire factory in Bangalore, Abdul lived with his wife, their daughter-in-law and two grandchildren in a shack near Reay Road sta-tion on the Western Line. "I saw that they were carrying out a survey," he said. "Since it was a large area of 880 households, a meeting was held and they asked us if we wanted to join, and I was very happy to join."

As a boy of fifteen, seeking adventure, he had run away from his home in West Bengal in 1957 with a bunch of school chums. In Mumbai, he got a job in the kitchen of a hotel, where he was paid with meals and a place to sleep. "In 1969, I went back to West Bengal," he said, "and married a girl, and came back to Bombay. We settled on the railroad, and I worked as a cook and caterer." Usually, he explained, he went to the house of the person throwing the banquet or party and prepared the food in their kitchen. "But I was also setting up in a makeshift tent," he said, "and cook-ing in there."

Madhuri and her neighbours also joined the Alliance, through Mahila Milan. "We started going to meetings in the Byculla office," she said, "then formed our own society and were even able to get 300 rupees each from the government to hire a truck to move our belongings." As the organization took hold, she said, many people stopped drinking, started saving money and looking after their families properly. Speaking from the Mahila Milan office in Lallubhai, dressed in a sari of deep orange, she said, "I think the people were really ready to have a change their lives."

As the apartment buildings were slowly constructed, the majority of railway slum dwellers lived in temporary transit camps set up and maintained by SPARC with World Bank funding. Once they were ready, meetings were held and decisions made collectively about which families would have units allocated to them. The criteria they used were based on practical considerations: the size of the family, the number of elderly or infirm and for some, the length of time they had been saving for such a move. To counter any accusations of favouritism, the whole process was kept transparent and out of the purview of local politicians hoping to score points. In some cases, the railway slum dwellers also arranged themselves into groups of fifty families, maintaining the same physical proximity in the blocks after they moved. Nonetheless, the transfer to Lallubhai Compound was difficult for many families, particularly the least prepared or those who had not organized.

Built on cheap, vacant land with no transport links, no ration shops to purchase subsidized food and fuel, insufficient places in the few existing schools for the influx of children and no recreational or green space, Lallubhai Compound was, in effect, a modern, new-built ghetto of the poor. It was one to which the members of the Railway Slum Dwellers Federation could either move, and start living in its suboptimal flats surrounded by dusty wasteland, or else spend several years in transit camps, waiting for something better. It is also a graphic example of what is wrong with so much official foreign aid, grants and loans.

It is only too obvious that the billions of dollars in overseas development assistance sent from rich counties to poor ones over the past decades have done little to alleviate poverty. David Satterthwaite of the IIED has written extensively about why so much apparent munificence fails to make much of a dent in developing-world poverty rates. "Not surprisingly," he wrote, "much of what is funded brings little or no benefit to urban poor groups." One of the first problematic characteristics he identified is that official aid agencies and development banks "were never set up to respond to the needs and priorities of poor communities. They were set up to provide 'recipient' governments with large capital sums (as grants or loans) and professional advice."

This has generated an enduring contradiction: often, the very people who have proven themselves either chronically unwilling and unable to deal with the plight of their nation's poor, or are hopelessly inept at doing so, are the ones who get to disperse vast sums of money intended for them. In fact, in countries like Brazil and Indonesia, not to mention a host of others, "recipient" governments actually cause or worsen poverty — as does the World Bank itself — through their economic policies.

What's more, these developing-nation government bodies, now usually referred to as partners, are of course political entities. Their priority is to stay in power (and often self-enrichment). What happens when funding is intended for communities, citizen groups or NGOs who do not support them, question their legitimacy or even actively oppose them and their policies? According to Satterthwaite, "no national government in Africa, Asia or Latin America will sanction increasing funding flows to institutions over which they have little control." And while, he said in a recent interview, this issue has been debated since the late 1960s, the model remains essentially unchanged. Obviously there does have be room for some government-to-government aid — villagers may build their own school or clinic, but they need their governments to staff and equip them — yet the emphasis on elite, rather than popular, decision-making needs new and profound scrutiny.

Average people in affluent nations are generally in favour of their tax dollars going through official development assistance agencies to help stem the scourge of poverty in the Third World. Yet all of the control over how those dollars are spent, over how or even if aid projects really might make a difference in the lives of the poor, is in the hands of people unaccountable either to the poor or to those original donors. "The people whose needs justify the whole development industry," wrote Satterthwaite, "are the people with the least power to influence development and to whom there is the least accountability in terms of what is funded and who gets funded." Rather, an edifice of waste, corruption and hypocrisy has been built precisely upon the backs of the world's most needy and destitute. Aid "watchers'" like ActionAid have found that many countries shortchange their own efforts, a phenomenon it calls "phantom aid." ActionAid's most recent study dates from 2004, a year when it estimates "that a massive $37 billion (47%) of the $79 billion in headline aid… was 'phantom,' while real aid stood at only $42 billion."

The bulk of that phantom aid went to technical assistance (a problem dealt with in the next chapter). Another big chunk of it is simply debt forgiveness, relieving local governments of the responsibility of having done nothing productive with their loans. Still more is actually spent on immigration-related expenses in donor countries and on administration costs. However, another reason that foreign aid rarely helps the underprivileged is that quite a bit of it is not meant for them in the first place. Rather than attacking the roots of poverty, it is destined to strengthen the capitalist structure that nourishes them, through economy-boosting infrastructure projects like highways, bridges, airports and dams. In some cases, large capital investments such as dams and airports end up escalating poverty by displacing local communities and destroying their livelihoods. Add to this the fact that so much official and bilateral aid is given with strategic political issues in mind; the so-called target groups — the desperate people we in the First World believe we are helping — are barely within the aim of the wealthy international institutions claiming to do so on our behalf. According to a 2005 study by Pekka Hirvonen for the New York-based Global Policy Forum, "Instead of allocating their aid based on where it is most needed, rich countries often favor recipients that are of direct political or economic interest to them. As a result, the most impoverished people of the planet actually receive less aid than those in middle-income countries."

Then there is the problematic issue of tied aid — loans or grants that are conditioned on the recipient nation spending much of that money on goods and services purchased in the donor nation. In the United States in 1996, for example, more than 70 percent of all foreign assistance was tied to spending it on more expensive U.S. goods. In 2009, it had decreased to 26 percent. A quarter of Canada's official aid had to be spent on Canadian products and services in 2007, a decrease from more than 40 percent in 2005. There has been so much controversy in recent years about First World companies essentially receiving huge percentages of aid money intended for low-income nations that the practice is gradually being dropped by some governments. Britain and a few other European nations untied their aid several years ago, and the Canadian government has committed to untying all of its aid by 2012.

Even so, the Canadian International Development Agency, or CIDA — the body responsible for the bulk of that country's $5 billion foreign aid budget — remains the target of heavy criticism on a number of fronts. With its policies dictated by the Department of Foreign Affairs and International Trade, the focus and priorities of CIDA are constantly shifting, heavily micromanaged and often contradictory. Decisions are based, therefore, not on humanitarian — let alone social justice — considerations but on the political advantages to be won by the Canadian government. The biggest recipients of Canada's foreign aid, for example, are currently Afghanistan and Iraq — two nations riven by war and corruption and notorious for the inability of average people to demand accountability or express their will.

CIDA's inner workings are neither transparent nor accountable, with annual reports to Parliament merely showing the amount it has spent in aggregate figures rather than the results, or effectiveness, of that spending. It takes CIDA almost four years on average just to approve a project. While the agency may well have many capable and altruistic people working both at home and abroad, in 2009, Canada's auditor general, Sheila Fraser, blamed its cumbersome bureaucracy for fifteen years of failure to implement aid effectively among the world's poor.

Another troubling aspect the big donors have long faced is the time frame constriction attached to projects. International agencies with large amounts of money have to spend it quickly within a project cycle and, in order to keep administration costs down, with limited and temporarily assigned staff. Yet as Satterthwaite has pointed out, "If, in the end, a lot of poverty reduction is changing relationships between the poor and local government, or the poor and outside funding agencies, sometimes it needs more staff time and less money."

So the focus has increasingly switched to giving foreign governments money to build their capacity, bolster their own development plans and foster better governance — as opposed to simply carrying out vaccination programs or constructing schools. Development bureaucrats call this SWAP, for sector wide approach, or "basket aid." Joint funding is provided by several donors, often in the form of budget support to, yet again, a recipient government and is geared toward a program or an entire sector rather than a project. "In theory, this removes the rather unrealistic time schedules," said Satterthwaite, "but it also means they're as distant from the reality of the local poor as anything else. In many ways, the aid agencies that shift the basket funding are further distancing themselves from the dialogue that's actually needed on the ground."

Indeed the paradox of "big" aid resides in how the kind of work that will have the greatest impact on communities of the poor is actually considered wasteful. "It is amazing what they can do," said Satterthwaite, "with $50,000 when it's them who decide what they're going to do with it, what local funding they're going to leverage, and which local government person they're going to bring into it." But for Stephen Brown, associate professor of political science at the University of Ottawa, "Giving out micro-grants — from the bureaucratic perspective — is just not effective. It's not a good use of resources." Aid professionals, he pointed out, are required to spend the same amount of time managing a project costing $50,000 as they do one that costs $5 million. As a result, said Brown, "with these big international organizations and bilateral donor agencies, there's something structurally wrong about the interface. It's just so hard to imagine that working well."

It is also extremely difficult to actually perceive the change brought about by government-to-government transfers and gauge the outcome. "So much of what CIDA and other donors do is working through governments and institution building," said Brown, "and there's just no way to know. And things like good governance. How do you measure that? So this desire to be able to catalogue the improvements that are the direct results of our own contributions — it just can't be met."

What about the smaller international NGOs, many of which do implement projects and have a higher proportion of their staff actually based in low-income countries? While some, like Oxfam, have been trying new approaches like asset-based community development — where poor communities begin the aid process by thinking about and listing their assets, whether those be plots of land and livestock or particular skills and the knowledge of elders — they face the same pressures as bilateral donors. Despite their diversity, in terms of both their development philosophies and the outcome of their work, in general they are constrained to keep staff costs low and project spending high. They are also often unwilling to take on risk.

In a 2008 study of sixty-one of the world's most prominent NGOs, researchers at Germany's Kiel Institute for the World Economy found that, by and large, their efforts did not complement the work done by official aid agencies. Rather than branch out and find those communities falling outside areas already receiving aid, or what the researchers called "difficult institutional environments," they tended to work in sectors and geographical areas where the official agencies were already present. They also tended to cluster, taking advantage of the same on-the-ground partners everyone else used instead of searching out new ones. And while they are located in some of the globe's neediest countries, collectively providing some $15 billion worth of funding annually, they also tended to choose nations "with common traits related to religion or colonial history. Taken together," they added, "our findings suggest that NGOs keep a low profile rather than distinguishing themselves from other donors and trying to excel under risky conditions."

When a project fails, or fails to meet their needs, to whom should the underprivileged of this world complain? In Lallubhai Compound, a great many of its new residents were unable to carry on the small businesses that had helped them survive in the slums. Those with jobs had to spend more money on fares and travel further to get to them. At the same time, their cost of living had risen steeply: there were taxes to be paid, water pumps and communal areas inside this arid complex to be maintained, electricity bills to be met. "And if you don't have kerosene," said Sharmila, giving another example, "you can't start a fire inside your house to cook your meal."

Neither the World Bank nor the MUTP — the sponsors and designers of this project — consider such picayune dilemmas their problem. Their goal was to build a structure and send the poor there so the trains could run more rapidly and a highway be made wider. So it should not be unexpected that many destitute people who are rehoused in such flats end up selling them and moving back to the street or slum.

Thus, the whole aid paradigm is so huge and unwieldy and fraught with other interests, that simply alleviating poverty is at the same time beyond it and too insignificant to be done directly. It has become, wrote Paul Collier in *The Bottom Billion*, "so highly politicized that its design is often pretty dysfunctional." For Sheela Patel, "in many ways aid providers are just tinkering, just trying to get the poor to manage their poverty better."

Nonetheless, the Indian Alliance recognizes the necessity of relating to and engaging with NGOs, government agencies and the development banks.

Indeed, since his early days in the Bombay Slum Dwellers Federation, Jockin has collaborated with a large number of local and international NGOs such as BUILD, Service Civil International, Care, CARITAS — even with Mother Teresa at the refugee camps set up in Kolkata during the Bangladesh war. Yet he considers the Alliance's leadership in finding solutions the platform on which stands its growing roster of achievements.

The experience of Janata Colony revealed that, like the individual police officers who would warn Jockin ahead of time that he was going to be arrested, the state is not necessarily a monolith. Another reason for the Alliance's success, therefore, has been its ability to seek out and find those individuals within government who will listen to and work with, rather than against, them. The Alliance recognizes that it must evolve a relationship with the state.

South African political scientist Mark Swilling has called this balance between negotiation and protest "radical pragmatism." In evaluating the strategies of the urban poor in the Shack/Slum Dwellers International, of which the Alliance is a co-founder, he considers the emphasis on direct engagement with the state "the most controversial and counter-intuitive" of its methods. "In situations where states have low levels of legitimacy (which is most places) this approach fuels the most heated accusations," he wrote, "of 'reformism,' 'cooptation,' and 'doing the state's work.' What the critics of radical pragmatism do not realize is that engagement achieves three things: it forces communities to clarify exactly what they want. It hones the skills of leaders who soon realize that what they get at the negotiating table depends on the strength of their organization formations on the ground." And finally, it wins "concessions that help sustain long-term commitments of... groups that must witness rewards for staying organized."

According to Sundar Burra of SPARC, "The poor say, 'don't alienate the state! We have to live with the state.'" It not only owns much of land on which the poor are squatting, it is also the body charged with doling out services such as water, electricity, health care and education. "The government tends to see us with good eyes, so to speak, because what we try to do is go to them not with problems but with solutions," he added. As Swilling has noted in South Africa, Sundar admitted that, "We have been sort of criticized for what is perceived as our close relationship with government because of this by some intellectuals. We say, that if you are an intellectual, you can afford an armchair, detached vision of the world. Our concern is what happens to the urban poor. Anybody who can have an impact on urban poverty is somebody we want to engage with. It can be a critical engagement — you don't have to buy into their overall perspective — but you have to negotiate and discuss. Our aim is to change *their* perspectives, *their* policies and programs without sacrificing our basic values."

Is it fair to equate the bringing of a solution to government to "letting the state off the hook?" Would the return to a more militant movement that challenges the state politically be an alternative? These questions underscore how the achievement of concrete improvements and decision-making powers over basic, even minor aspects of living conditions can be of greater impact for the poor than a change in government through elections. The taking of power by reformist, leftwing parties in nations like Brazil, for example, have shown that a switch at the top is no guarantee of change at the bottom.

"We are trying to renegotiate the rules and the relationships between government, NGOs, community-based organizations, international institutions and United Nations agencies," said Sundar. "How to we do that? By organizing the poor to build their capacities and bring their voice into the debate, and I think that sanitation is a good example, where roles and responsibilities have changed. Before, the municipality built them, people had no role, and they almost always collapsed in a year or two. Even with issues like education or health," he added, "how can people participate in the running of their local schools or clinics? The old government strategy is one where everything comes from above, from some politician, some bureaucrat or some mayor. There is always someone else running the show. But our participation in a democracy should not be limited to just voting every four or five years."

In fact, promises of political change have delivered little to the poor of low-income nations, and they are often very aware of this. As rank-and-file members of the Indian Alliance often pointed out, politicians make promises but, when elected, move out of the bounds of accountability. In Dharavi, for example, when the state government announced that it was going to begin rehabilitating the slum, scores of organizations, political parties and even private developers came in and began encouraging slum dwellers to set up societies and cooperatives to get in line for new housing. As the bureaucratic entanglements this implied, however, started bogging them down, these groups fell apart, their former members more suspicious than ever of outsiders.

So while poverty is certainly political, members of the Alliance do not see traditional politics as the route to take in bringing about the changes they want in their lives or society. Appadurai calls this "its vision of politics without parties." The Alliance will negotiate with whichever party is in power, but its membership is no politician's automatic vote bank. In fact, members are not permitted to use the organization or its resources for any political party or to stand for election (although as Sundar has pointed out, as individuals, they are free to do so.)

Rather than organizing for political reforms, members of the Alliance do so to pressure for, achieve and manage change through series of concrete goals. They consider their role in managing services as crucial to this, whether it be maintaining the slum's communal toilet, participating in community policing or building their own homes. The decentralized structure of the Alliance and the way decision-making is handled constitute two more aspects of a more direct and participatory democracy than that offered by neo-liberal governments. Membership in the Alliance is part of an endeavour to wrest control of policies that have an impact on the urban poor away from the political and social powers-that-be, from governments and NGOs. No doubt many of the latter may feel that the people with whom to negotiate are the Alliance's more high-profile members. Yet, says Jockin, "I tell the government, 'don't talk to me! Go and check with the people!' And people are empowered through this decision-making process, which is around issues. When one issue is resolved, another one is already cropping up."

In Lallubhai Compound, the disadvantages for its new residents have been balanced by the security of their new homes — and even by differences as esoteric as the fact that families were able to arrange better marriages for their daughters. Yet it has been through organization in the Indian Alliance that residents have found ways to solve new problems. Members of both Mahila Milan and the Railway Slum Dwellers Federation continued to advocate the importance of savings, but more importantly perhaps, of meeting to discuss problems and how to solve them. Madhuri Kisan Karat, for example, worked on the loan committee of her local Mahila Milan branch, and as she put it, "It's not like just this writing on a piece of paper. I go to meet people who need a loan, talk to them directly to find out why and so on, all kinds of things."

Her branch had also set up a program called Poverty Line. "With Poverty Line we are going to each and every building, finding those people who need help," she said, "and donating basic food and kerosene. None of the political leaders are interested in helping. So as an organization that has been going on for many years now, we are handling most of the issues ourselves. People here as a community can decide how to solve the general problems, what to do and what not to do."

Meanwhile other railway slum dwellers, like the Karim family, were still waiting to be housed. "Over all the many years we've been living on the tracks," said Mr. Karim, "I've always been afraid that some day the municipal authorities would come and demolish our structures. So we required someone to give us some support, and I feel we got that. I also hope that some day in the near future I will be provided with habitation through the organization." To that end, Abdul Karim's society was saving up an impressive 10,000 rupees a day, ready for the time when they would have to start paying for the utilities they had always just taken. For him and for the rehoused poor in general, organization implies the difference between being stuck out in the middle of nowhere and starting a new life in a distinct part of the immense city that is now their home. "The organization has been reaching to almost every corner of the city," he said. "There is hardly any settlement that has been left untouched by the organization, but in case there is any that has, we will try to reach out to them too."

• 6 •

Women Together

Laxmi Naidu is back in her old neighbourhood of Nagpada, collecting cash into the small cloth bag hung within the folds of her flamingo-pink sari. She is a small, dark woman of fifty-one, with a slight overbite and a manner that comes across as both animated and self-possessed, the demeanour of someone who has lived through a great deal. We have taken the train from Mankhurd, travelling in the ladies car, second-class, for a four-rupee fare. It is jam-packed, hawkers worming through us all with boxes of hairclips and packets of *bindis*, the double row of ancient ceiling fans whirring away like crazy, but imperceptible nonetheless in the clammy heat. Emerging at Byculla station, we take a short taxi ride through the crowded streets with their building-supply stores and cheap eateries, past a street of closet-sized rooms, each with a bed inside, their doorways flanked by brightly garbed women with oiled hair, their faces painted as vividly as plaster saints. "This red letter district," Laxmi explains with her courageously erroneous smattering of English.

We stop at Peer Khan Road and walk into a squalid colony of pavement dwellers, 248 families whose huts encircle the walled yard of a school compound. Beyond a large and fetid heap of rotting garbage, hopping with crows, a compact line of jerry-rigged huts begins, one hard by the other, so that as soon as I take a step past one family at their open doorway I am already at the door of another. It is as if the trash has followed us, to cling to the mottled walls, scatter itself around the doorways and pile on to the roofs of these mostly wood-slat hovels, except that everything I see — the bits of clothing and battered pots, the tattered bedrolls and old plastic barrels — has some value for someone.

Inside are dark spaces that would make a bus stop seem roomy; while there may be an elevated shelf of electrical appliances and fans, there is little these can do to dispel the claustrophobic heat and depressing obscurity of the interiors where they belong. Right beside the garbage dump an old woman is sitting outside on a cart beside two lolly-gagging grandsons. I ask how long she has lived like this, and one of them translates the bleak response, "All her life."

Laxmi, meanwhile, is occupied, standing calmly, notebook and pen in hand, within the milling population of the slum. Housewives in saris and skinny young men in long-sleeved shirts and cotton trousers run up to her waving bills; they have been expecting her. She puts the money into her cloth bag and opens her notebook, carefully writing down who has given it, whether it is for repayment of a loan or deposit in a savings account. Around a corner, the row of shacks and their accompanying visual mayhem continues. A diminutive, worried-looking man named Mohammed Ansari hands over one hundred rupees, paying down a loan, he says, that he used to buy the equipment needed to start up a pattern-cutting venture. Children of every size are jumping up and down all around us like a swarm of grasshoppers, and Mohammed's wife Mahatum yells at her two boys to stop, so they can talk to me. Across from us is their two-storey shack, which, hard as it is to visualize, they share with their family, Mohammed's mother, brother, sister-in-law and *their* two children.

Heading back down the way we first came in, Laxmi brings me to the spot of now-vacant sidewalk where she lived for twenty-two years. There is a piece of pale blue-painted metal sheeting bent into the chain link fencing and a pile of reddish earth in the gutter of the street. She makes little squares with her hands; here was the spot for washing up, there the bed, taking a few steps and making a sawing motion to show where its outer wall stood. Behind us is a small dusty park where, she says, people would go and sit at night to relax.

Laxmi came to Mumbai from Andhra Pradesh in 1974, at the age of 17, fleeing a job she both hated and feared, as a domestic servant in a brothel. She travelled alone, unbeknownst to her parents. "My parents didn't even know I had left the house," she says matter-of-factly, "nor did I inform them. My parents were always fighting; my father was a drunkard and always beat my mother, and I did not like this."

Arriving in the city, Laxmi put together a shelter on the sidewalk in Byculla and once again found work as a servant. Yet as a young girl on her own, she was aware of how dangerous her situation was. From her hut she used to observe a group of men working on a construction project, she says. She noticed that one in particular seemed honest and serious; he didn't drink or get into fights, just concentrated on doing his job. His name was Satyanarayan Naidu and she asked him to marry her. "I said, 'I want to marry you,' and he said, 'okay, but I can't give you a good home because I am just a worker. So you have to adjust,'" is how she remembers the proposal.

A painter, Satyanarayan had a friend who worked in a barbershop and let them sleep in it overnight. The couple's first child, a daughter named Sundita, was born there in 1978, but by the time Laxmi gave birth to her second child, a boy named Rajesh, the building housing the barber shop was torn down and the family found itself living on the sidewalk again, on Peer Khan Road.

Across from us is the once-elegant, now ramshackle, apartment building of grey stone where Laxmi worked as a servant. Because of this she was allowed to fetch water there, but only at 4:30 in the morning. She cooked her family's simple meals of rice, dal and vegetables inside her hut. "A lot of people do it outside," she says, "but it's not safe. Some light their fires on the road, and there are accidents. So I cooked inside the hut because my family was small."

It was not long after her return to the pavement, however, that Sheela Patel came into her life. Working at Nagpada House community centre, Sheela found schools and day care for the children of the pavement dwellers so that Laxmi, juggling two jobs by then, would leave Sundita there every morning. In 1984, Sheela left Nagpada House because, she said, "the organization was not ready to defend the rights of pavement dwellers." She and the group of friends who founded SPARC moved to a garage behind the local dispensary, across the street from a patch of park called Jhulla Maidan.

That same year, a new problem had come up for the families living on Byculla's sidewalks. One day, says Laxmi, "an order from the Supreme Court said that all of the pavement dwellers' huts would be demolished, because we have to make Bombay a better city. So Sheela came and asked us, 'after the Supreme Court order, how are you going to stay and where?' And we told her, 'we have no idea what we are going to do.' So Sheela said, 'why don't you all join us? We are going to help you.'"

Beyond a sympathetic ear and the facilities of the office, SPARC had few resources to offer; it was, as Sheela described it, "a joint exploration of what was possible." Or as Laxmi recalls, "the pavement dwellers would have to do the work themselves."

She and four other women began to meet frequently at SPARC, which aroused the curiosity of her neighbours. "The people were very inquisitive," she says, "so they started asking us, 'where are you all going every day?' And we said, 'we go to Jhulla Maidan office.' When people asked why, we would say that, after the Supreme Court's order, all our huts are going to be demolished and we don't know where we are going to stay, but Sheela is going to tell us, she is going to show us a way, so that's why we go there every day. So they said, 'can we also join?' And we said, 'why not?'"

More and more women began attending the meetings at SPARC, discussing their problems and finding common cause. Life on the sidewalk, they felt, was harder on them and their children than on the men, who would leave every day to work. They were women together, and when the NSDF and SPARC encouraged them to create a formal organization, that is what they called themselves in Hindi, Mahila Milan.

One of their first concerns was getting their hands on government ration books that subsidized basic foodstuffs. The first timid group of women was all but thrown out of the ration office, but they informed themselves — by law, everyone in India has the right to a ration book — and insisted. Armed with this knowledge, their clamouring and shabby appearance embarrassing the office staff, the women finally got them. Heading back to the slum waving the precious documents, they began a small revolution, as droves of women started going to the ration office and getting their books.

Meanwhile, eviction notices began to arrive, along with the usual stickwielding police. They were met by women and children in a large group, surrounded by curious passers-by. The women told the police that they would dismantle the huts themselves and get rid of any rubbish and, says Laxmi, "because of our collective strength, they didn't demolish." This, she said, gave them "bargaining power with the government," even as the families rebuilt their huts in the same place the following day.

On later visits to municipal offices, she adds, "we didn't mind telling the government that even though we were poor, we were not thieves or doing anything wrong. We just don't have a place to stay. And no one will give us loans because we don't have money to pay them back."

Ever since Mohammed Yunis established Grameen Bank in Bangladesh in 1976, banking for the poor has assumed a mantel of reverence bordering on the religious among poverty alleviation and development experts. On the one hand, it is a concept that recognizes that the poor can use and repay small loans — often more promptly than the middle class or rich — to vastly improve their paltry incomes through small business ventures. By providing infusions of cash to purchase productive assets, micro-finance has undeniably allowed millions of poor people to make incremental or even sizeable improvements in their wellbeing and that of their families. It is also considered a major factor in the empowerment of women in low-income nations; identifying an apparently greater sense of responsibility to the household, micro-finance institutions have particularly focussed on women as the ideal recipients of small, short-term loans.

On the other hand, not all micro-finance schemes are created equal. Hundreds of organizations around the world — from the Programme d'Appui aux Mutuelles d'Epargne et Credit in West Africa to FINCA International Village Banking in Latin America — exist to encourage savings and offer credit to the poor. Some establishments are not-for-profit, while others, like Mexico's Compartamos or India's SKS Microfinance, are for-profit, selling shares on the stock market and thus delivering part of their borrowers' interest payments to outside investors. Many large institutional banks maintain micro-credit sectors and there are even websites, such as

Kiva or MicroPlace (a subsidiary of EBay) through which average folk can extend loans to selected recipients with a mere click of a mouse. In all, global micro-finance has an estimated 113 million clients and assets of $22 billion — figures that are likely on the increase.

A problem arises, however, with the growing tendency to place micro-credit in and of itself on a pedestal, to consider it the only mechanism the poor need to pull themselves up by their own bootstraps and leave destitution behind. Behind it lies the notion that a market-led development approach is more efficient (and less costly) than attempts by the state to alleviate poverty, more realistic than outright charity. It is only partially true and easily skewed to suggest that the solution to global poverty simply rests upon the financing of a billion potential street entrepreneurs; taken as a be-all and end-all, it can have dangerous consequences.

A study on the limits of micro-credit by Jason Cons and Kasia Paprocki of the Goldin Institute identified a number of concerns with some of these micro-credit schemes. Information collected from a survey they carried out in Arampur, in northern Bangladesh, where eight micro-lenders were operating in a village of just 1500 people, found intimidation and physical abuse common among the field officers when loans were not paid back in time. Dependency on additional loans was trapping people in deepening spirals of debt. Even the price of dowries had become greatly inflated be-cause of general knowledge about the availability of credit. What's more, the notion that micro-credit represented the best solution to poverty meant that other forms of support previously provided by NGOs had disappeared. "In Arampur," they wrote, "microcredit has replaced other NGO-provided rural services and, as many told us, eroded long-standing safety mecha-nisms within the village. Many reported that during the hungry season, they had no choice but to use loans for the purchase of food." For the researchers, there was a risk in the uncritical adoption of micro-credit and market-led development initiatives. "This risk is compounded," they wrote, "by the systemic failure of many micro-finance institutions to engage the communities where they work in the process of designing and evaluating micro-credit programs."

Although the structure of their savings circles is similar to Grameen and others that set up groups of peers to oversee savings and loans, the Indian Alliance sees what they are doing as very different. "Grameen Bank is build-ing money," said Jockin. "It is addressing financial issues, not the issue of change."

In the Alliance, members take loans from a collective of which they are a part and to which they feel an immediate responsibility. Within these support groups, lenders and borrowers discuss the purposes to which the loan is to be put and how it will be repaid. However, it is the great emphasis placed on what they call "daily savings" that has, in many respects, become the organizing core of both Mahila Milan and the NSDF.

When members of the Alliance talk about saving, wrote Arjun Appadurai, "it becomes evident that they are describing something far deeper than a simple mechanism for meeting daily monetary needs and sharing resources among the poor. They are also speaking about a way of life organized around the importance of daily savings, which is viewed as a moral discipline... which builds a certain kind of political fortitude and commitment to the collective, and creates persons who can manage their affairs in many other ways as well."

Whether putting aside a few rupees every day or extending small loans to each other, saving and banking can seem paradoxical when carried out by people who live with such constant need. Yet as a railway slum dweller named Jyoti Pujari explained it, her husband, Uday, "earns about 100 rupees a day. Usually for about 50 rupees, I could buy what we needed to eat. And the rest my husband would spend on this and that, on cigarettes, or betel leaf." This meant, she concluded, that instead of buying both, he could only buy one or the other and the remainder was put into her daily savings account.

Mahila Milan first set up what they called a crisis credit fund that made small loans when a family was experiencing some kind of emergency — a medical crisis or their sale goods being seized by the police. While this got families out from under the terrifying power of the city's many moneylenders and their exorbitant compound interest rates, the fact that they were meeting and dealing with these crises also got them planning for and finding better solutions to them, such as starting a dialogue with the police and local authorities on street trading. Yet the whole point of the emergency credit scheme was to have a mechanism that would protect the funds they were slowly accumulating towards their dream of a decent home.

As Mark Swilling has written, "If what is needed is a model of self-organization within communities that is easy to replicate, appropriate to a reality that effects everyone no matter the context, flexible enough to adapt to specific circumstances and is not dependent on external leadership of professionally managed systems, then organizing around cash (savings and loans) makes enormous sense.... It is also an approach that is in some ways remarkably appropriate to the specific realities of developing country cities, where daily contact is possible in highly congested communities where living, working and recreational spaces get merged together into a seamless web of complex adaptable dynamics."

For Swilling, there is another difference between savings circles and what he refers to as "the high-cost, top-down control model inspired by Grameen, and the exploitative model practised by many micro-credit organizations." Aside from the trust and solidarity that is built up among members of the savings circles, their money stays within the community. Members have access to credit from their pool of collected savings, but interest payments are also channelled back into it, instead of into that of an external micro-finance institution.

By 1987, their savings growing, Mahila Milan became qualified to receive loans from the Ministry of Women and Child Development in Delhi; the loans were used to start up small enterprises, from vending to carpet repair to recycling. Hundreds of women were now discussing and deciding matters such as interest rates, the creditworthiness of the borrower and the viability of business plans. As new groups from other parts of the city and other regions came to Byculla for on-the-job training in accounting and organizing, it was someone like Laxmi who would teach them.

"I don't just speak to people but actually take them out and make them realize the actual situation on the street," she says. " I give the bag to them and ask them to collect money and put it in the bag, then write down who is giving how much. Then I would take them back to Byculla office and tell them to put the savings amount under the savings column and the loan amount under the loan column so that the correct amount was under the correct column, and then on the computer also. And then people realize that it is not very difficult to do. It is actually easy, if you give it a try."

Nonetheless, the streets around Nagpada still had to be cleared, and housing remained foremost on peoples' minds. As their savings grew, the members of Mahila Milan began actively searching for land on which alternative housing might be built. "Every time we told the government, give us places to stay," says Laxmi, "they'd say 'there is no land.' So we went around the whole of Bombay, even though we didn't have money, finding these plots of land, and once we found these plots, we told the government, 'here is a plot and we want houses on it.'"

The members of Mahila Milan also decided to design the kinds of flats they wanted. What the Slum Rehabilitation Authority offers a slum dweller, when it offers anything at all, is a 225-square-foot apartment, ten feet in height, in a standard seven- or eight-storey high-rise. But, says Laxmi, "in each house on the pavement, there are two or three generations living, so we asked, 'how can we stay together?' We didn't have enough space for all the people in 225 square feet, so we decided to have another floor." This elevated the height to fourteen feet. "First we measured it out using our saris," she explains, "then put up the model and it was passed by the government."

In fact, they devised four different models with various associated costs. Mock-ups were made with cardboard and cloth, and in March 1988, these were put on public display. Government representatives, the media and slum dwellers from all over the city were invited to come and have a look at them, introducing a new feature to the struggle for housing that was to become commonplace in Mumbai and other Indian cities. Along with their festive public inaugurations of new, clean and locally managed toilet blocks, Appadurai has called these celebrations of the possible "a democratic appropriation of a statist and middle-class consumer model which became very popular in India in the 1980s."

Bringing together their peers as well as authorities, they are both social and political events that place slum dwellers on a level ground with the people who, to all extents and purposes, control their conditions. If the building of a shack in a slum or on the sidewalk is the mark of destitution and exclusion, of one's inability to join the middle class, then the displaying of house models born out of the creativity of the poor suddenly reverses perceptions. They exhibit not only the slum dwellers' technical and planning abilities, but their humanity. And they offer neighbours and other slum dwellers a vision based on reality, opening discussions about design, construction materials and costs among those for whom a proper home is still an utterly abstract desire. As Appadurai has described it, "Through this process, their own ideas of the good life, of adequate space and realistic costs were fore-fronted, and they began to see that house-building in a professional manner was only a logical extension of their greatest expertise, which was to build adequate housing out of the flimsiest of materials and in the most insecure of circumstances. These poor families were enabled to see that they had always been architects and engineers and could continue to play that role in more secure housing."

What did these flats look like once actually built? Laxmi was by then living in an apartment on the third floor of a four-storey building of eighty-eight units in a place called Milan Nagar, in Mankhurd. Like the buildings in Dharavi, it was designed to keep maintenance costs down to 200 rupees a month per family. There was running water for one hour a day, communal toilets at either end of the corridors on each floor and no elevators. On each floor, though darkened and enclosed, the corridors bore uncanny similarities to the streetscape, replicating its use of space. Doors were left open to visitors, the thresholds hung with wafting curtains; children ran around and played on the steps. Some families kept goats in the hallways, tethered to doorknobs and placidly chewing grass while reposing on the shiny plastered floor. Overhead, strings of red-and-green paper flags with crescent moons and stars — every family in the building but Laxmi's was Muslim — crisscrossed the ceiling.

A picture of Sai Bhaba, the same orange-garbed saint I had seen in the cart pullers' sidewalk shrine at Alankar Chowk, greeted visitors from Laxmi's door. Inside, light beige walls and the tall single window in the open kitchen area kept her apartment naturally bright and well ventilated, reducing her dependence on electricity. Narrow stairs led to its upper half-loft, and its only enclosure was the small washroom. On the wall near the door was a framed black-and-white photograph of a solemn-faced man, a *tilak* of sandalwood paste on the glass over his forehead. "My husband," said Laxmi in English, pointing at it.

The women of Mahila Milan were allotted the land for this and three other buildings in 2001, fifteen years after the initial eviction scare, and for two years oversaw its progress to ensure they were getting good quality material. Adding up to about $7 million, construction costs were met with a complex blend of savings, government subsidies and loans from local banks guaranteed by international aid organizations. With her daughter then married and living in Hyderabad, Laxmi and her son Rajesh took possession of the flat in 2003. It was several years too late, however, for Satyanarayan, who died in 1996.

It was a few years after their marriage that Laxmi was finally reunited with the family in Andhra Pradesh she had fled so many years earlier. By the time her two children had been born, she said, she decided to write and tell her parents that, while she was a Brahmin, she had married a man of the *nai*, or barber, caste.

"I wrote to my parents to tell them that I had a married a person who eats non veg," she said, "and that I too had learned to eat non veg. I said, if you will agree to it, I will come home to visit; if you don't agree, I will not come. So my mother wrote and said, 'it doesn't matter, we just want to see you.' That is how I went back home. And that is how I learned that after I left, of course my parents were also worried about me, because they had been searching for me."

Her afternoon's work finished, Laxmi heads for the Byculla office where the cash from Peer Khan Road would be counted, registered and stored before being taken to the bank. Jhulla Maidan still has straggling rows of brick and tin shanties beneath a few trees, its slum children playing cricket on the blasted patch of earth as if nothing could be more satisfying than a well-hurled bowl or a taken wicket. Inside the shelters, men sit at their sewing machines and outside, women sell kitchenware and shoes from large squares of plastic.

A group of little girls approach as we arrive, looking around and doing what children often do there, first stand and stare almost in awe, then spring to a kind of engagement action, moving around to catch my attention and trying to say something in English. Usually only one or two are able to do so.

These little girls are dressed in *salwar kameez* of dazzling colours but noticeably secondhand. The heat has pressed strands of hair against their foreheads and pinked their cheeks. They seem bright and happy, but anyone might wonder what kinds of lives they will have, growing up in a society where being female counts for so little, where only rarely will they have a say in important decisions, access to a proper education or any recourse if the male authority figure in their lives mistreats them. And then the true immensity of what the women of Mahila Milan have attained strikes me. The leap from illiteracy, dependency and super-exploitation to essentially running their own bank, negotiating with authorities and building their own apartment buildings is so vast, the simple listing of all they have achieved can never be sufficiently indicative of what that really means.

Yet inside the SPARC office, which is quite small and has grass mats on its cement floor, there is no sense of historical significance. Women are coming in, down-to-earth and businesslike, with their collections of cash and their chatter. A tray of tongue-burringly sweet chai does the rounds as the talk remains focussed on what Laxmi's neighbours have managed to accomplish and the rest of them will someday as well: a new, clean flat they can finally call home. As Laxmi's neighbour Sangira Ansari put it, "It is such a big thing to obtain a house of our own, that we feel this is our strength, and because of that we want to tell people to join. There are lots of people like us and we should support them."

In 1991, the Indian Alliance decided to go global, sharing its strategies with the South Africa Homeless Peoples Federation (an organization renamed the Federation of Urban Poor in 2005 and in the process lending itself the wonderful acronym, Fed-UP), which had constructed more than 13,000 housing units by 2007 and secured tenure for 20,000 more families. In 1996, they and four other similar organizations came together in the Slum/ Shanty Dwellers International, or SDI, which currently has federations or affiliates in thirty developing nations across the Global South. A potent example of grassroots globalization from below, this ever expanding network connects itself through cheap modern technology like the internet, trades and exchanges ideas and experiences, and has not only collectively saved but manages millions of dollars.

Finding common ground across all kinds of language and cultural barriers, the fact that society's most disadvantaged people have constructed such a network is remarkable. Thus, the SDI has taken people like Laxmi from the streets of Mumbai to countries like Thailand, Cambodia, the Philippines and Kenya, and taken people from slums and shantytowns in those and other countries to India.

She could understand, said Laxmi, the initial reluctance of her impoverished counterparts to believe that there was anything they could do to better their situation. "We tell people," she said, "that even we didn't believe that this organization could benefit us in so many ways, but that after joining, we have witnessed what benefits we have got. So that is why we are here to tell you all and to explain it to you all. Then, people slowly start developing trust in us. They say, 'when these people have come from so far and they are talking to us, it means that there is something we are going to get, not now, but later on after organizing and forming our own Mahila Milan.' So that," she concluded, "is how people formed the groups outside of this country."

It is also people like Laxmi, rather than outside experts, who orient and train new members in census taking and mapping, micro-finance and model house exhibits. For the poor, this kind of teaching and learning method turns a vital switch. As Swilling has pointed out, "not only does this enable people to learn new things from other places, it also deepens self-understanding via the process of telling one's own story to others."

In traditional aid projects for the poor, external experts almost always take on the roles of teaching and advising. In fact, the Organisation for Economic Co-operation and Development exempts technical assistance from its current policy of discouraging tied aid among its members. Since so much overseas aid nowadays is made up of such assistance, or "human resource transfers," the move to untie aid can, however, be seen as largely symbolic. Various nations that have untied their aid still choose among their own in the search for consultants.

What's more, these consultants don't come cheap. Along with salaries, travel, moving and living expenses, most even require "hardship allowances" for being in the Third World in the first place. In his paper produced for the Global Policy Forum, Pekka Hirvonen estimates that their fees — which amount to $1000 a day or more — can eat up as much as a third of the original grant or loan funding. "Overpriced technical assistance," he wrote, "is a form of inefficient aid that is closely linked to tying. In 2003, an estimated $18 billion… was spent on technical assistance, mainly on consultants advising and supporting recipient governments." In 2002, in Cambodia alone, he pointed out, "aid donors spent an estimated $50 to $70 million on 700 international consultants — an equivalent of the salary of 160,000 Cambodian civil servants."

According to David Satterthwaite of the International Institute for Environment and Development, "Many consultants reproduce similar analyses and proposals regardless of the country they are in, precisely because their knowledge of each location is limited." Based on what he has heard from project managers in certain low-income nations, he added in a recent interview, "I know that in the case of the multi-lateral development banks, a very substantial part of the budget disappears to consultants, that (the recipients) didn't choose, giving advice they don't agree with." As a result, he said, it is the poor who are paying for "sub-standard advice" to wealthy professionals, who, in many cases, know far less about how to resolve their problems than they do.

While the University of Ottawa's Stephen Brown has pointed out that in some cases, such as land-mine removal, a global expert with experience in other countries is the best option, organizations like ActionAid see technical assistance as another way for wealthy nations to maintain control of the aid agenda. They even note that as far back as 1969, the Commission on International Development chaired by Canada's former prime minister Lester Pearson found it did not do much to further "either national or global development objectives." ActionAid's research finds that technical assistance fails to build long-term capacity, reduce poverty or even recognize "that development is an indigenous, locally driven process."

For the Indian Alliance and other similar organizations of the urban poor, therefore, their persistence in defining and driving the development process represents a near-revolutionary change. "Instead of relying on the model of an outside organizer," writes Appadurai, "who teaches local communities how to hold the state to its normative obligations to the poor... there is a heavy emphasis on methods of organization, mobilization, teaching and learning, which build on what the poor already know and understand."

The political message is that, as a poor person, you are able to bring about change in your life, and your partners in this great venture are other poor people like you. Identification is not with a politician, a political party or a charitable organization but with your neighbours, your class and, increasingly, with similarly disadvantaged and unjustly treated people around the world.

Ranging in size from a few hundred to several hundred thousand, some decades old and others less than a year, all of SDI's affiliates share a common belief: that organizations of the urban poor must play a defining role in the way in which governments and multi-lateral agencies discharge their obligations to them. They are pioneering a third path between two other types of organizations that work with or among the poor: confrontational, rights-based mobilizations attached to trade unions or leftist political organizations that often dismiss the significance of negotiation to win concessions, and establishment development institutions that prefer to avoid confrontation so as not to jeopardize such concessions.

Over the past few years, federations in, or groups affiliated to, the SDI have also had access to an international fund for both housing and micro-finance projects. The International Urban Poor Fund is managed by the SDI board and routed through the International Institute for Environment and Development; its monies come from private trusts, the Norwegian Agency for Development Cooperation and the Swedish International Development

Agency. Disbursing almost $5 million between 2001 and 2006, the Fund's methods can direct resources to the organized poor themselves and in doing so highlight much that is wrong with traditional aid (as explained in the previous chapter).

According to Satterthwaite, the International Urban Poor Fund has four distinct advantages over development money that goes to national and local governments. Rather than financing projects or sectoral reforms that may contribute only indirectly if at all to poverty reduction, he said, federations apply for small grants to support either savings groups or housing iniatives. Because organizations of the poor take charge of developing and managing the project, "they make sure funding goes as far as possible by pushing down unit costs, by adding their own contributions and by using the funds to leverage additional support," he wrote in a recent issue of *Environment and Urbanization*. In some cases, grassroots groups have constructed housing or improved infrastructure for as little as one-seventh of the cost of conventional projects, as they come up with solutions professional developers haven't thought about.

The Fund is also flexible in what it supports and where. "This means," wrote Satterthwaite, "that it can respond to opportunities and priorities identified by local groups — and do so far more quickly than external funding organizations." What's more, there is no fighting over, or competition for, funding. Decisions about what gets funded are not only based on immediate need but on other "smart" criteria like a project's potential to catalyze other development processes or to boost newer, less consolidated federations. The relationships between the people who decide on funding and who request funding are horizontal, rather than flowing downwards from those above to the poor below.

Finally, the availability of this funding to an organization of slum or shanty dwellers has certain value-added aspects. It can be the element that pushes the hand of local government to sign off on legalizing tenure, to put in much-needed infrastructure or to pay for the construction of housing. But it also shows both government and potential donors that the organized community is a partner they can work with, as opposed to a disparate horde of illegal squatters, in need of professionals' help because they are unable to help themselves.

The urban poor organized in the SDI are providing multi-lateral development agencies and donor governments with a valuable template they should be using; they have, yet again, come up with a solution to the bleeding away of aid money into the pockets of the corrupt and that does nothing — or woefully little — to stem the tide of poverty.

Through their participation in this continually expanding organization, millions of poor people are both contesting the status quo and engaging with a state that is increasingly unable or unwilling to deal with the social and economic injustice that lies at the root of poverty. While recognizing the complex nature of the state, the poor are collectively insisting on making its multitudinous voices heard and taken seriously. Those voices are, over time, growing ever louder and more evocative, as they articulate the desire to make decisions, take on responsibilities and bring about long-term change.

Part 4

Argentina

• 7 •

Sí o Sí

L uis Romero was wandering the streets one day looking for scrap cardboard to sell when he ran into Pascual Nievas, a man he used to work with at the Wasserman steel mill in Villa Martelli, a suburb just outside the city of Buenos Aires. It was raining, he recalled, just starting to grow dark and the cardboard he'd already gathered was getting soaked. Pascual, who ran the strapping machine at Wasserman, recognized Luis, although he hadn't seen him in over a year, not since he'd been let go after working there for nine years as a welder. That was in 2001, and as the months went by, Luis's attempts to find a new job had left him with nothing but his daily searches for scrap to sell to a recycling depot in the city. With a wife and four children to support, what he managed to earn depended on what he managed to find, the equivalent of five dollars on a good day, much less on the worst.

Since the end of the 1990s, picking through refuse had become the main fallback for ever larger numbers of former industrial workers, yet Pascual found it difficult to hide his emotion. Remembering his skills in the pipe factory and how hard he used to work, "Pascual couldn't believe I was doing what I was doing," said Luis.

For Pascual and the other fifty-five workers then remaining at Wasserman, *cartoneando* as they called it, was the ominous spectre of the future that continually confronted them. Most of them were older workers, with more seniority than those let go, yet they had only basic education and skills no longer valued. If the circumstances were tough for the younger workers, for them, not yet at retirement age, they were terrifying.

At one time mill owner Ignacio Wasserman had employed as many as 250 workers, who produced 12,000 tons of steel tubes, pipes and panels a month. The firm once had branches in Cordoba and San Luis as well, but the business began to founder badly in 1998, as the Argentine economy headed into recession. As more and more staff were laid off, simply going to work became hugely stressful, Luis recalled. "We wouldn't talk to each other, not because we were angry with each other, but because we were so aware of who would be let go that day, always wondering, 'whose turn is it? Who is going to fall?'"

"But the real blow," said Pascual, "came in 2001. Businesses closing, the desperation of people, all of this during the government of De la Rúa."

Diana George, who had worked as a bookkeeper in the mill office since 1966, also remembered those difficult months very clearly. "The company owed a lot of money by 2000," she recalled, "most of it to the banks and to Siderar," the steel monopoly from which Wasserman bought his raw material. Then, in February of 2001, Siderar loaned the company $2 million worth of steel. "We were very happy with that," she said, "because it was 2000 tons, and we had work. Suddenly, in June or July, there was nothing with which to pay the debt charges nor the other purchases, and we still owed the $2 million to Siderar."

For Diana, then fifty-six, the fact of the missing money came as a huge shock. With short, neatly coiffed grey hair, her glasses on a string around her neck, she came across as motherly, even though she had never married or had children, and somewhat staid, correcting herself whenever a rude word threatened to burst out of her mouth. "There are no words to describe the anguish you feel when you know they are lowering your wages and it's not enough to live on," she said, shaking her head. "I can't explain it; it's terrible." Diana found herself borrowing from her brother-in-law to make ends meet, overcome by a sense of shame and fear for the future that made her physically ill.

In October of that year, Wasserman told her and the other remaining workers that he would pay them the equivalent of $25 a week just to stay home. "A pittance," said Pascual. "But we wouldn't accept that. We came here every day, afraid he wanted to empty out the factory, but not really knowing what was going to happen. We came because we were afraid of being out on the street."

By then there was no longer any work to do, and over the following weeks, the workers passed the time playing cards, kicking around a soccer ball and chatting amongst themselves. Every day they made a big cauldron of soup, with everyone contributing either a few pesos for ingredients or a chunk of meat, the leftovers packed up to take home to their families. "And with every day that passed," said Pascual, "our desperation was greater. The country was falling to pieces. "

It was, however, during those days of waiting and worrying, of idle conversation, that the idea of forming a cooperative and taking over the mill arose. "The moment arrived," said Pascual, "where we stood there and talked about whether we could do this thing, and not lose our source of employment."

Looking for any information he could find, Alejandro Coronel, who had also run a strapping machine, punched the words "*fabricas recuperadas*" into a search engine on an office computer and came up with references to what by

December was starting to become increasingly common. Among the articles on workers taking over their workplaces, he found the name of Luis Caro, along with his phone number. "We called Dr. Caro," said Pascual, using the common title for lawyers in Argentina, "and he came over right away."

Even so, there was perhaps more doubt among the workers than decision. A stocky man in his late fifties, his short greying hair neatly cut and combed, Pascual recalled that at one point he asked: "Dr. Caro, with all due respect, I don't know if I'm crazy or you're crazy, but how are we even going to pay the electricity bill here when we can't pay our bills at home?' And Luis Caro said, 'you have hands? Well, put your hands to work.'"

And in the end, Pascual summed up, "there was no other alternative. We had to make this work, *sí o sí*. And God help us."

In Spanish, *sí o sí* means yes or yes; there is no yes or no, no maybe, no other option. It was a phrase used repeatedly by members of the many co-operatives set up in shuttered or abandoned factories barely standing among the ruins of a dysfunctional economy. From auto parts to ice cream, health care to leather making, workers across a broad spectrum of economic sectors faced their fears of uncertainty, the worries of their families and the scepticism of the business class, to assume the difficult path towards democratic self-management. In the attempt to explain their decisions, *sí o sí* became a kind of theme, one that illuminates the motive behind something as socially revolutionary as it is pragmatic. As Peter Ranis, a City University of New York professor emeritus and long-time observer of Argentine politics, described it, "The recuperation of bankrupt factories and enterprises is creating a societal movement within a neo-liberal economy that combines elements of worker entrepreneurial capacities with a resurgence of collectivist solidarity and working class consciousness."

Yet how could such a thing have happened — in Argentina of all places? A model of modern, pro-market economic policies, the world's fourth-largest exporter of food, it strikes few as a developing nation at all, especially Argentines themselves. With its beautiful, cosmopolitan capital of Buenos Aires, large middle class, high standards of education and distinctly European culture, probably no other country could offer a greater visual contrast, at least, to all the others described in this book.

Unlike Mumbai, there are no huts leaning precariously over its streets or women cooking meals on its sidewalks, no cart pullers or head loaders struggling to move heavy burdens with their own physical strength. Its shantytowns, or *villas miseria*, cling to the urban periphery, far from view. The United Nations' human development index puts Argentina up at number 11 in its list of 135 developing countries (where the Czech Republic is number one and Afghanistan number 135), placing it well above India at 87 and even Brazil at 42. At one time boasting the seventh-largest economy in the world, no one was fully prepared for the truth of Argentina's political and economic vulnerability in 2001.

This dire state of affairs, however, had not come out of the blue. Decades of government policy, especially during the presidency of Carlos Menem, had gradually left it with an impoverished industrial base, high unemployment and mammoth debts. Rather than invest in productive enterprises like manufacturing, Argentina's capitalist class found a new way to make money: the financial markets. Based on the privatization of state-owned companies, International Monetary Fund loans and inflows of cash from emerging-market investors, economic activity had begun to resemble a pyramid scheme, with business owners sending the ensuing profits out of the country and the government continuing to borrow. Such schemes also necessitated an over-valued peso, pegged at par with the United States dollar, making exports less competitive than ever.

As the economy crashed in 2001, Argentina not only defaulted on its $141 billion public-sector debt payments but a further $21 billion owed to foreign bondholders. Cut loose at last, the peso took a nosedive, losing two-thirds of its putative value, and banks barricaded their doors to prevent a run on savings accounts. As gross domestic product shrunk by 15 percent, over a fifth of the working population found itself jobless. Between May 2001 and October 2002, the percentage of Argentines living below the poverty line almost doubled, from 35.9 to 61.3 percent, and the number of indigents rose from 11.6 to almost 30 percent. The poorest 10 percent of the population was receiving only 1.4 percent of national income, while the richest 10 percent was taking in 37.4 percent. What's more, while the top 10 percent of income earners received five times that of the bottom 10 percent before Argentina's military dictatorship, by 1991 it was fifteen times, and by 2003, forty-four times. While prior to 1998, Argentina's GDP per capita stood at over $8900, by 2002, it had fallen to just $2500, the same as that of Jamaica.

Thus, in a nation not traditionally associated in people's minds with poverty, the inequalities that had always been there, that had fuelled the popularity of Juan and Eva Perón and their championing of the *descamisa-dos*, or shirtless, were hugely exacerbated. In poor northern provinces such as Tucumán — where an estimated 64 percent of the population lived in extreme poverty — Misiones and Santa Fe, children were soon dying of hunger. Desperate Argentines ransacked supermarkets and, in one celebrated case, swarmed an overturned cattle truck on the highway outside Rosario, hacking pieces of meat from dead and dying livestock. A doctor at a hospital in Tucumán, where sixty children suffering from severe nutrition were being admitted each month, aired his frustration: "This is not Africa," Oscar Hillel told *The Guardian* newspaper in November 2002. "This is Argentina, where there are 50 million cattle and 39 million people — but where we have a government that is totally out of touch with peoples' needs."

While many countries have long struggled to shake off the legacy of colonialism and raise their income levels, it was as if Argentina had somehow embarked upon an opposite course, one that took it from relative prosperity to destitution via military dictatorships and neo-liberal economic policies. Even the reliance on scrap picking as a livelihood, so common in places like India, became a suddenly graphic indicator of urban poverty as, in Buenos Aires alone, an estimated 100,000 people had resorted to it by 2002.

Protesting against a system that clearly wasn't functioning, hundreds of thousands took to the streets in cities throughout the country, forcing President Fernando de la Rúa to resign on December 21. Three more equally hapless leaders followed in the space of a fortnight. A nation that had always considered itself more European than South American had fallen into not only economic but political chaos.

Out of this debacle, however, like desert flowers after a rainstorm, social movements suddenly bloomed. All over a country where radical politics were considered an anachronism and consumerism the object of devotion, millions of people were finding their inner militant. According to James Petras, "At the high point of the popular mobilizations in 2002, analysts estimated that between two and three million Argentines participated in some kind of popular protest."

The new legions of unemployed — and now unemployable — organized themselves into radical protest movements of *piqueteros*, or picketers. At one point numbering as many as 200,000, they marched and demonstrated, attacked banks and threw up blockades of burning tires, their demands spanning the immediate, such as food and welfare money, to the entire social transformation of the nation.

These mobilizations, in which at least thirty-three people were killed as police attempted to quell the rioting, cut across classes and sectors in Argentina: just about everyone had something to lose. No longer invisible, the poor had hit rock bottom, unable to even feed themselves. The industrial working class had lost all hope of ever seeing bi-weekly paycheques again. The middle classes were furious at the loss of their savings, jobs and opportunities and a future for their children. As Andrés Ruggeri of the Centre for the Documentation of Recuperated Businesses, or CDRB, has described it, "The perception that life projects and the much-promised possibility of a rise in social status — that dream of a grand and empowered Argentina that had enraptured generations — had disappeared."

Among the newly mobilized were the thousands who joined neighbourhood associations through spontaneous, on-the-street meetings where both individuals' and the nation's predicaments were discussed. Many of these so-called popular assemblies started to organize barter groups, soup kitchens, the distribution of milk to children, the planting of vegetable gardens in empty lots of land and anti-establishment cultural events. These constituted as much an indication of the poor's knack for collective problem solving as an illumination, perhaps, of the depths of penury to which the populace had sunk.

And with the entire structure of capitalism questioned by vast numbers of people, support for the notion of workers taking over their workplaces to save their jobs — as well as a host of community services — was also generalized. What for workers was this question of *sí o sí*, for the popular movements, the politicians, the press and their neighbours — pretty much the same people who had repeatedly voted for presidents offering neo-liberal recipes — capital and private property had been defrocked.

The first workplace takeovers, however, came before the vivid upheavals of December 2001. Like canaries in a coal mine, these workers and their factories constituted the first evidence of the country's corrupt and mistaken economic course as well as harbingers of the form of resistance to come. One of the earliest factories to set itself up as a cooperative was Union y Fuerza, a copper pipe plant in the Buenos Aires suburb of Avellaneda. It had gone bankrupt in 1999, and its forty-eight remaining workers spent almost two years trying to claim the plant for themselves before re-opening it in January 2001.

South of the capital, in La Plata, a similar situation impelled the workers of the Union Papelera Platense paper plant to set up their cooperative. They had also spent almost two years trying to claim the wages and benefits owing to them after the company went under. Its cooperative rebooted production in April 2001.

In November, two plants, in Quilmes and nearby Berazategui, were taken over by their workers. And at the end of the month, the workers at the Zanón ceramics factory in Patagonia turned a new page in the history of their struggle for labour rights and, ultimately, workers' control of production. They had begun to press for general assemblies and democratic union representation back in 1998, when their boss, Luigi Zanón, fired a hundred workers. Although his business had received free land, tax exemptions and millions of dollars in subsidies, Zanón still owed creditors $75 million. As the workers had succeeded in voting in an alternative union slate in 1999, Zanón — who once congratulated Argentina's military rulers for keeping the country safe for investors — responded by locking out the entire workforce of 250 in November 2001. The workers' response, in turn, was to not only occupy the factory but to garner the support of entire communities in the city of Neuquén for their actions. Under the slogan, "A worker-managed factory at the service of the community," they leafleted and connected to a variety of groups and sectors, public service workers, the unemployed, students and local churches, all of which supported the objectives of the Zanón workers. This support and its high level of class consciousness stood as a bulwark against police raids, the jailing of demonstrators and numerous legal challenges, as the plant began production again early in the following year. By 2005, a further 170 workers had joined the cooperative, which had changed its name to FaSinPat, for *fabrica sin patrones*, or factory without bosses.

In the case of Wasserman, its owner declared bankruptcy on the 4th of December that year. On the 20th, as protest marches rocked Buenos Aires, more than a dozen died and President de la Rúa finally resigned, Luis Caro won legal recourse to the steel plant by offering to pay its bankruptcy trustee a thousand pesos a month in rent. And while Ignacio Wasserman himself scoffed at its chances, telling them, "You'll need at the very least a million dollars just to start," the plant would from then on be run by its workers, impoverished as they were, united in the newly named Los Constituyentes Workers Cooperative.

If one were to search for what some social scientists refer as to as the framing mechanism — the interpretation that allows the poor to stop blaming themselves for their own poverty — in Argentina, it was capitalism itself. The depression and the social convulsions to which it gave birth were impetus enough for many workers to not only think about taking over their workplaces, risky as this seemed, but to find the support of sympathetic workers in other industries, in members of the middle class who saw what they were doing as good for the very nation and to a certain extent, members of government.

In 2001, said Natalia Polti, a sociologist and CDRB researcher, "it was seen as a good thing to recuperate the source of employment." Not only did workers engaged in the struggle for self-management find a favourable ear in the media, she said, they also quickly learned to zero in and put pressure on "those legislators who would bring about expropriation laws."

What's more, two pillars of labour reform had, by this time, fallen. Along with the lack of support for industry, the governments of the 1990s had also dismantled the social safety net. Even those lucky enough to get severance payments or welfare — about $50 a month — could barely survive and were no longer finding paid work to replace them. Indeed, the fact that companies were seeking creditor protection or declaring bankruptcy meant there was no money for severance payments at all. As Julian Rebón and Ignacio Saavedra point out in their book, *Empresas Recuperadas*, "The disappearance of established legal compensation for sacking, and the lack of payment for indebted salaries, are key elements in the gestation of the (workplace takeover) process."

The other broken pillar, of course, was Argentina's unions. The nation's largest, the General Confederation of Workers, or CGT, had largely allied itself with Carlos Menem and the Peronist Party during the 1990s, at the same time as it slowly lost power and members, thanks to successive lay-offs and the entire policy of de-industrialization. An opposing federation, the Argentine Workers Central, or CTA, provided some alternative but at a remove from the workplace itself, as it dealt increasingly with the unemployed.

For Luis Caro, the unions had in fact become enemies of the workers, "forcing them," in his words, to take wage cuts and accept lay-offs. "Unionists have become so bureaucratized that they don't even attend to the workers anymore," he said. "The unions have lost the confidence of the workers." Caro based this assertion on the many times unions attempted to stop workers from going on strike for unpaid benefits or from taking over their workplace. On this point, Rebón and Saavedra agree. "The workers' actions met with indifference and abandonment on the part of unionists," they wrote, "above all when the conflict was clearly directed toward the takeover of the company. The loss of union clientele moving into a cooperative; the loss of business and economic possibilities with business owners after bankruptcy; or just the lack of vision of the unionists anchored in their traditional practices, led more than one union to not support, and in some cases, even oppose the workers."

The National Movement of Factories Recovered by Workers, or MNFRT, did not form itself until April 2003. Electing Luis Caro as president and Alejandro Coronel as vice president, it included auto parts, food processing and textile plants, foundries, tanneries, a bakery, a day-care centre, two hospitals, the maker of Grissinopolis *grissines*, or breadsticks, found on every restaurant table, and the Navales Unidos shipyard. Some of its eighty member cooperatives had participated in an earlier organization, the National Movement of Recovered Enterprises, or MNER, set up during the very early days of the wave of workplace bankruptcies and takeovers that would reach a kind of critical mass in 2002.

The MNER brought a highly politicized and class-conscious approach to the issue of factory recuperations yet, in doing so, seems to have alienated a large number of cooperatives. Its main leaders, left-wing lawyers José Abelli, Eduardo Murúa and Diego Kravitz, had what Caro called, "a more ideological-political analysis of the issue, and so there was a break." Or as Gregorio López, president of a cooperative called Lavalan and the MNFRT's secretary, explained it, "We were following the same ideal, which is to serve our comrades, but we don't have a commitment to any political sector. Yes, we do politics, which is to recuperate factories."

Two other matters helped bring about the split from MNER and subsequent formation of the MNFRT. One, according to Gregorio, was the fact that its leaders assumed a position of representation without a clear directive to do so from the cooperatives. "For me, personally, it was a bomb when José Abelli, Eduardo Murúa or Diego Kravitz would appear in the media speaking on our behalf," he said. "They would say, 'I am president of the National Movement of Recovered Enterprises.' When did we elect them?'"

Located in a gritty Avellaneda neighbourhood of old brick factories, many of them closed, Lavalan sorts, washes and combs raw wool mostly destined for export. Bales of clipped wool, much of it still tangled with dirt, twigs and burrs, come in and then go out as neat coils of greyish fibre, ready for dying and spinning. Its original owner's son, Juan Carlos Fanton, effectively closed the business in 2001, declaring the company bankrupt in December. On strike over unpaid salaries and other labour debts since December 1, the remaining twenty-five workers (accused of "acting like Cubans" by their union) set up their cooperative on January 4, 2002, and won expropriation the following July.

In September, however, it was surrounded and attacked by mounted police on the orders of a judge, responding to a former Lavalan client demanding the return of his wool. The cooperative argued that the wool had been listed as part of the business assets and refused to budge. They were supported by a large group of people; the workers' families were joined by neighbours, the local popular assemblies, some *piqueteros* and workers from ten other recuperated factories, including Los Constituyentes. The entire expropriation process had taken months of interviews and audiences with judges, Avellaneda city officials and members of the provincial legislature. There were many times, said Gregorio, when he and others would show up for a court appearance only to be told that a leader from the MNER had assumed responsibility for their case. "So we decided to leave and form another movement," he said. "And they tended to see this as a betrayal."

Yet another, more critical, difference existed between the two groups: the method — and the political interpretation underlying it — of the takeovers themselves. It is perhaps not surprising that in 2001, the traditional left of Argentina believed that workers were suddenly ready to storm the barricades of capitalist exploitation, backed by popular discontent within a context that saw so much, if not just about all, of the system utterly discredited. And yet, as Esteban Magnani pointed out, the workers "just wanted to turn around what they considered an unfair situation, and were practically forced to take over the factory to do so."

"Concretely," said Caro, "we never agreed with the methodology they used (in the MNER), for example, the slogan 'Occupy, Resist, Produce.'" This slogan had been borrowed from the Landless Rural Workers Movement in Brazil, where the constitution recognized the right of peasants to claim unproductive or state-owned lands. For Caro, in the workplace recuperation movement, "the issue of occupying is a strategic error." The legal system, he pointed out, did not come with a social conscience. To simply occupy and take over the factory is considered a criminal act and sent to judges dealing with penal law, which they have to observe in their deliberations. His advice to workers seeking to claim a workplace in lieu of unpaid wages and the right to gainful employment (which *is* recognized in Argentina's constitution) has been to go on strike. They then do have the right to occupy their workplace, converting the action from a criminal case to a labour issue.

"In the system in which we live," said Caro, "there is an entire juridical scaffolding that preserves private property. I agree that property should have a social end, but that doesn't exist in Argentine law," he said. And while he did not agree with the system, he added, "for now that is what there is."

So in the case of Brukman, a company that made suits, its cooperative spent almost two years trying to survive, was evicted three times and spent nine months camped out in a tent on the street surrounded by 80 police. The mostly female workforce was owed huge sums in back wages, and in the weeks before the riots of December 2001 had been receiving little more than bus fare. Yet, said Caro, "they had never declared themselves on strike. It was, 'since the owner hasn't come back, the owner abandoned it, this is for the workers.'"

The December 19 Cooperative, as it was christened, had been supported by Argentina's Socialist Workers Party, or PTS, which campaigned to have the business nationalized by the government — with no success. For Magnani, the needs of the fifty-two seamstresses, pattern cutters and pressers "came second place to the vision of the PTS, which was to transform the cause of Brukman into a national one, to show that capitalism is unviable and unde-sirable, and that workers should work for the state." The workers, he added, "felt they had the right to a job, while the PTS believed that the state should run the means of production."

Caro was called in after the third eviction and, within three months, succeeded in having the factory expropriated by the provincial legislature and turned over legally to the cooperative. While he said that he could not understand why the left did not consider taking over workplaces through the procedure of a strike when the law allows them to do so, it seems clear that its preference has been for a far sharper challenge to the capitalist system.

The idea that the working class should own and manage the means of production has certainly inspired many hundreds of Argentine workers in the broader factory takeover movement. They have found not only a different understanding of their own value as workers but an ideology that proposes a different society, one based not on individual profit but the fair distribution of resources among the poor and working class. The problem the left in Argentina faces is its interpretation of working-class liberation from exploitation, its adherence to the idea of the state running the means of production *on behalf of* the workers.

The member cooperatives of the MNFRT have no desire for the state to become their new boss. In numerous interviews, their members made it clear that they wanted to run their own workplaces, take their own decisions and divide among themselves the fruits of their labour. The huge risk involved in claiming and taking over a workplace, then turning it around, has thrown up distinctly pragmatic paradigms. These workers began their journeys in conditions of severe penury and debt, both as individuals and as producers. They not only needed to embrace a completely different working process but be enabled by it to take home a certain amount of money every week to support their families.

For the traditional left, these are examples not of the workers' victory but of failure; the December 19 Cooperative is just making suits, not changing the world. As a result, the cooperatives in the MNFRT remain highly autonomous, scoffing at the accusation, put about by many of Caro's detractors, that it is he who tells them what to do. Pointing out that it would be impossible for one person to run some 120 cooperatives up and down the considerable length of a country like Argentina, they also place heavy emphasis on the centrality of their general workers' assemblies.

Within the MNFRT, every cooperative divides its earnings equally among members, regardless of the jobs they do or responsibilities they take on. Presidents and entire administrative councils are subject to recall at any time if the assembly decides it is warranted. The fact that every worker is not only aware of, but intensely interested in, expenses and income, would make it practically impossible for anyone to gain ascendancy over the rest of their comrades. Paramount to their sense of independence, decisions made in the general assembly always trump the opinions of their council president.

Early on a weekday morning in mid-November 2007, I made my way to the second-floor salon of the Hospital Israelita, in the Caballitos district of Buenos Aires, where a cooperative of 130 had been running the institution for the past three years. A general assembly was taking place, with Luis Caro and about twenty others sitting around a large oval table; extra chairs and benches were ferried in and arranged in front of it and along the walls. Combining some big issues — Caro's explanation for his presence — as well as plenty of small ones, the meeting would run for a good two hours or more. Throughout it, more and more staff came in and cast about for seats, rolled in office chairs, delivered whispered messages and left again, the continual demands of the hospital itself intruding on the morning's lengthy agenda.

The bustle and stir of the medical workers in their multicoloured uniforms contrasted with the salon's chandeliers, old-fashioned arched windows and ornately framed commemorations, illustrating the very history of the venerable institution itself. Now slightly shabby, the lofty, wood-panelled room was a kind of throwback to another era, one reflecting the optimism and dynamism of the city's Jewish community, refugees from Russia, Germany and Poland, who had both sustained and frequented the hospital. It had been founded in 1921 by the Ezrah Jewish Association for Welfare and Mutual Aid. This association had "channelled the creative spirit of a very strong community," cooperative secretary Paulino Quintana told me later, "and grew thanks to its contributions."

Comprising two wings and seven floors, the massive art deco–style building took up most of a city block, housing not only the wards and operating rooms but a nursing school, the offices of its own health insurance scheme, called Isramed, and over a dozen out-patient clinics offering services from dermatology to nuclear medicine. The doctors, researchers and teaching professionals who worked there were considered among the best in Argentina, said Paulino. A tall, thin man with cropped greying hair and a prodigious supply of energy, he had begun working in the personnel department while still in his twenties. He seemed inordinately proud of the hospital's prestigious reputation, lowering his gaze and taking a tone that suggested I might think he was exaggerating but he was not. The Hospital Israelita, he asserted more than once, "was one of the best hospitals in Latin America."

Yet over the latter decades of the twentieth century this glory had started losing its burnish. As recurrent economic problems took its toll on the entire country, donations dropped off and the hospital board often found itself unable to meet its payroll and bills. In 1979, the Ezrah Association declared "a serious economic emergency" and made a public plea to the Jewish community for help. By 1997, the 1300 staff members had been shorted in their wages and benefits for so long, they went on strike for almost three months. Even though the hospital was busy, treating 4000 patients and more than 35,000 out-patients every month, it depended heavily by then on subsidies and loans from Banco Mayo, which was itself near collapse. Constantly afraid that the hospital would simply shut down, everyone from doctors to cleaning staff was taking home salaries of a few pesos a week.

Instead of closing, however, a shake-up took place, with a new board of directors transforming the ailing hospital, according to Paulino, from a non-profit to a for-profit. "Rather than orienting its efforts to the good of a community with special pricing and acts of solidarity," he said, "a group installed itself here that was more interested in commercial ends. And who paid the consequences were the workers."

Their union, the Health Workers Association of Argentina, or ATSA, was in full compliance with the new plan. "Instead of attending to us, it yielded to the bosses," said Paulino. As salaries fell yet again and hundreds of medical staff left, the hospital sought creditor protection in 2001, and finally declared bankruptcy on September 6, 2004.

Then, together with the former directors, ATSA decided to set up a cooperative. According to Paulino, "Their idea was to buy the hospital for a fraction of its worth, and of the 400 of us still working here by that stage, 70 people would stay, just their shop stewards. It would be a cooperative, but with other ends."

After much discussion, the hospital workers decided to confront this administration inside the main offices and, as cooperative president Eleonora Berton put it, "throw them out." Someone called a local twenty-four-hours news program called Cronica to come and film the proceedings for television. "What was with us all the time was that we wanted to stay in the hospital," explained Eleonora. "We just didn't know how, how to do it legally."

The following day, various lawyers including Caro, who had seen the conflict with the union the previous night on television, were invited to a general assembly of a few hundred workers. According to Paulino, they knew about the factory recuperation movement, "but this was a hospital, and it's rather complicated." Caro brought along with him members of a few of the recuperated factory cooperatives he had advised, and their input was decisive. "We said to ourselves, if another cooperative can do it, then so can we," said Eleonora. While the new worker-run cooperative received judicial permission to operate the facility on November 6, 2004, many challenges remained.

Neither Paulino, nor Eleonora, who usually chairs them, said much during the 2007 general assembly I attended. Rather, Claudia Gargiulo, a former nurse and now the administrative council treasurer, did most of the talking, beginning with the announcement of how much money the cooperative had in the bank: just under 16,000 pesos — about $5000. A series of exclamations of concern greeted this information, followed by spontaneous questions regarding what amounts this included, what might still be owing — or worse, to be discounted.

"What about the money from PAMI?" asked one, referring to the government-run social service for pensioners. "Is that in there?" Glasses halfway down her nose, Claudia consulted her sheets of papers. "No, but that's not due until the end of the month," she said.

At the same time, a new blood counter was needed in the lab, its cost, US$6500, eliciting gasps of shock. Then came an item on X-rays. At 20 pesos, the price they were charging was the lowest in the area, said Caro; should they raise the price or keep it low to attract more business? Everyone voted to keep it at 20 pesos. An item on whether they could hire more nurses lasted for almost half an hour, while another on whether to replace the billing system — a suggestion from Caro — was quickly discouraged by the staff, who said that while old, it worked perfectly well.

A red-haired woman in a lavender uniform named Liliana grew annoyed with a technician named Miguel over an ongoing problem with a sterilizing machine. He had called someone to come in and make an estimate, said

Miguel shyly, but no decision had been made. "Well, how am I supposed to do anything when we're always saying we have no money?" asked Liliana.

"Yes, but you ought not use that kind of tone with the *compañero*," said Caro. "This is a cooperative and we all have to take on responsibilities or it won't work."

"Well, I feel like you are both criticizing me," she countered.

"No. No one is criticizing you," said Caro, "but the machine has to be fixed. Sending material out to be sterilized is also very expensive."

By the end of the meeting, however, talk turned to the following Friday, the third anniversary of the co-op's difficult birth. "Sandwiches and soft drinks?" asked Caro, once the venue and who to invite had been settled. Through it all, Claudia kept the same equable demeanour, while Caro, frequently interrupted by his cell phone, made suggestions — "Shouldn't you keep the curtains to the insurance office open so it looks like we're in business?" — asked questions, answered questions and calmed things down when the discussions became heated. He had not been to a meeting at the hospital for two or three months, he told me later, the reason for his protagonism at this one.

Perhaps it was not surprising that, as Eleonora admitted, "every time we have doubts, we ask Luis — although we are loosening ourselves from him little by little." An operating room nurse, she had become the cooperative's president — very much against her will — when its initial administrative council had imploded after less than two months. The membership had accused it of corruption and collusion with ATSA, and its first president, Dr. Silvia Gallo, resigned.

"It was just before New Year's Day," Eleonora recounted, "December 30, to be exact, and I had been working all day. I finally got home and at 9 or 10 o'clock that night, I got a phone call from the *compañeros* here, asking me if I would agree to become the new president. I didn't want to at all, I was afraid to. But my mother said to me, 'You can't let your co-workers down at a time like this. They need you.'" The pressure on Dr. Gallo had included anonymous death threats "from the union," said Eleonora, and soon she too was receiving phone calls. "People saying 'we're going to throw your dead body into a ditch,'" she added matter-of-factly.

A blond woman with plump florid cheeks and a gravelly voice, Eleonora still worked in the OR when needed. "This has been something entirely new for me," she admitted, "to go from a closed place like an operating room to administering a hospital. It hasn't been easy." She had to learn to read legal documents, argue the cooperative's case in court, negotiate with suppliers and the Ministry of Health and, she told me, "not to say too much, just the right amount, and to listen first and then say what you are thinking. And then relate all of this to the assembly."

Paulino had also been reluctant to take on the position of secretary and deal with money, he said, "because of all the complications and conflicts that can come with that. But I was convinced that it was the only alternative we had in our lives at that moment."

Under worker self-management, the abandoned hospital had slowly but steadily begun to return to what it once was. Room by room, floor by floor, walls were painted and floors cleaned, beds reassembled and more patients taken in. Wages had gone up from 400 pesos a month to 1200, and 150 doctors came back to run their own clinics. "This is one of the great recuperated workplaces," said Dr. Federico García, an eye specialist. "Now that it's run by its workers, it functions well. Actually, it functions very well."

Caro's role had developed from that of adviser and cheerleader to resource of last resort, an assurance for the cooperative that, as far as the big picture was concerned, it was doing what it should. It was in large part this sense of security, said Eleonora, that allowed the cooperative to concentrate on the labyrinthine details of running and improving such a complicated institution, while adhering to Health Ministry standards.

Compared to the many years of conflicts and insecurity, of not knowing what or even if they would be paid, or when they would be fired, managing the hospital was not all that difficult for the cooperative members — and certainly less stressful, said Paulino.

"It used to be you got up in the morning and said to yourself, 'what's going to happen today?' And this is the part I love, where you measure the social consequences, because there have been *compañeros* who, because of the previous situation, have died. One had a heart attack. That feeling of impotence as you stand in line for your pay and when you finally get to the window, they say, 'sorry, there's no more money.' Those are the kinds of things that don't happen anymore," he asserted. "Even if there were to be a shortage of funds one week, what is there would be equally divided up and shared among the members."

While both Paulino and Eleonora agreed that the cooperative members were still learning to work without orders from a boss, the process of democratic decision-making was working. "The assembly is sovereign for us," said Eleonora. "In the assembly people decide, discuss, give opinions and add up all the different ideas toward a common objective, which is how to make the hospital bigger and better. That is the idea. So it's a challenge but it's also a question of animating oneself. We've had things go right and things go wrong. But here we are. Here we are, growing little by little."

Even in the midst of another recession, this one brought on the country by the financial crisis in the United States, patient numbers in 2009 were continuing to rise. More wards had been refurbished and nursing staff hired. "Things are going very well for us," said Eleonora. "We haven't needed to call Luis Caro for several months now."

· 8 ·

A New Dynamic

By November 2007, Argentina's economy was booming. Due in large part to high agricultural commodity prices and exports buoyed by a free-floating peso, the nation's GDP was growing by an average 9 percent annually. A new president, Cristina Fernández de Kirchner, had just been elected, taking over from her husband, Néstor Kirchner, after his four-year mandate. And with the apparent turning of the recession page came the gradual fading away of most of the social movements it had created.

As unemployment fell from over 20 to 12.5 percent and poverty levels from 53 to 33 percent, many in the unemployed workers' movement found jobs, however ill-paid. Many of the popular assemblists no longer had time to go to neighbourhood meetings, and the siren call of a new, more socially just order no longer found as much of an echo among the people. While media like the *Economist* and the *Wall Street Journal* had criticized Néstor Kirchner as a left leaning populist, he had in fact come from the same Peronist Party as Carlos Menem. Garnering just 21 percent of the popular vote, he had only won the 2003 election when Menem, slightly ahead in the first round of voting, dropped out. Emerging from a crisis some believed had elements of "a pre-revolutionary situation," the left not only failed to make electoral gains, it also failed to make itself relevant to the majority of the workers in the takeover movement or to the working class in general. Perhaps, with the worst of the crisis over, those social movements with no concrete goals or purpose simply began to disperse. Or maybe, in the words of Natalia Polti of the Centre for the Documentation of Recuperated Businesses, "all that effervescence that existed in the beginning was not well channelled." Yet for the member cooperatives of the MNFRT, the effervescence continued to bubble.

At the Navales Unidos shipbuilding cooperative, workers were negotiating a new long-term contract with a United States shipping company. The Nueva Esperanza cooperative making breadsticks had just won the right to the Grissinopolis trademark, allowing them to emerge at last from the jobbing they had been doing for several years for other biscuit companies. The former Ghelco ice cream factory, where the workers had begun production by selling the stacks of paper and cardboard left behind when it closed, had opened a showroom to attract new clients. In general, the cooperativists were taking home salaries of 1500 to 2000 pesos a month, about $500 to $650.

Meanwhile, a line-up of rattling trucks idled their motors on the street outside the green iron gates of Los Constituyentes, and Pascual Nievas was proud of their being there. "Did you see all those trucks out there?" he asked, as he crossed the drive from the offices towards the plant. "They're all waiting to pick up orders. They're waiting on us."

Inside the factory, a long noisy machine called an Otomil welder was drawing in a single shaft of steel, its massive bobbins forcing it into a curve, and that curve into a pipe, as clay-coloured water bubbled and sparks flew from the soldering mechanism that seals the join before it is cut to length. There were men watching its computer screen, removing the scrap and operating the guillotine, as the pipes were cut to size and deposited into large piles, ready for pick-up. They would be going to other local industries, Pascual explained, to be used in plumbing, swimming pools and gas lines. Throughout the cavernous hundred-metre-long plant, more machinery was spitting out other kinds and sizes of pipes, or cutting panels that would eventually form the sides of a refrigerator or stove. Someone else now worked the *flejadora*, or strapping machine, that Pascual had run for thirty years, while he spent most of his time searching out both new clients and supplies of steel.

While they didn't have the million dollars Ignacio Wasserman said they'd need to re-start production, other recuperated factories lent them a few hundred. From the office computers, cooperative members had found the names and addresses of past clients. "A group of the boys went out to talk them and said, did they want piping, that if they brought in the steel, we would make it," Pascual explained.

This kind of arrangement is called *"fazon"* in Argentina, one where the buyer supplies raw material and workers are essentially selling their labour, rather than a finished product. Jobbing was common in the early years of the factory recuperation movement, a symbol of the determination of its thousands of members to see their cooperatives succeed. According to Diana George, their first order was for 400 tons of piping and panels a month, and their weekly salary amounted to no more than 20 pesos. While such orders paid very little, in the case of Los Constituyentes, said Pascual, "it was how we paid the electricity. It was how we began to grow, to put together our small capital to buy our own raw material."

Los Constituyentes managed to survive its first three years by working *fazon*. There was no frustration or fighting over these small sums, said Pascual, "if otherwise we didn't have a single peso? We were all living the same situation, without a peso in the house. We all lived this process."

It was a few months after they began production again that he ran into Luis Romero in the street going through the garbage, looking for cardboard.

Things were still tough, the cooperative barely on its feet, but he made Luis a promise that as soon as there was a job for him, he would give him a call. Two months later, Luis got that call, and the offer of three days' work. A week later, he was called again, and this time got a week's work. A month later, he was brought back full time and made a co-op member.

"We began with fifty-six," said Pascual, "and as we have grown, we've gone about rescuing comrades who were fired by Wasserman and were picking cardboard in the street. That is why we are ninety members here today."

By then those workers were producing 7000 tons of steel parts and taking home salaries of 2000 pesos each month, with access to interest-free loans of thousands more. Slowly building up their supply of steel had finally released them from the necessity of jobbing, and soon they would be putting in a second shift, said Pascual, "because we have so much work to do."

A few other changes had been introduced in the plant. One was a cafeteria, offering a free hot lunch and allowing the workers to eat all together instead of alone at their machines. Another was a greater flexibility in where they worked. The cooperative's workers had essentially figured out how to run the entire plant, rather than just their individual machines, said Pascual, "by learning from each other. Today somebody can go and work in another section because there's a more fluid relationship among the *compañeros*; people explain things to each other better. Maybe we never did that before because we didn't have the opportunity."

This flexibility within the workplace, the recognition of the value of their shop-floor knowledge, is present in many cooperatives and can be seen as an element of empowerment among the workers. As Diana explained it, there was "a new dynamic. We've moved from a relationship of dependence, of simply taking orders, to telling yourself, well, now the decisions go through me, and not because of someone telling me what to do; it's what I say and what I do. It's something," she admitted, "you never quite get used to." While an invisible wall had previously separated her and the office staff from the plant, she said, "Now you collaborate with what you know best. But you can also put in your two cents' worth in other areas, your experience, your opinion. One isn't boxed in."

The greatest change, however, was in the way decisions were made. As millions of pesos were passing through the hands of the office staff, reduced from some fifty workers under Wasserman to just a handful, one of the main weekly tasks was printing up the details of every sum that came in and went out. These were read out at the weekly general assemblies. "How we did that week, how much we donated, how much we sold, how much we brought in, how much we purchased, how much we paid in electricity, and how much did we lend to you, or to you, or you," said Pascual. "Everything is transparent."

Aside from this — and suggestions, for example, on donations of goods to local schools — much of the discussion had been about growing their bank of steel. Siderar, burned by its relationship with Wasserman, had only been willing to give them 150 tons a month on credit. Instead, Pascual came up with the idea of buying steel from third parties offering far better credit options.

"He may not have a diploma or a high school or university education," said Diana, "but in the end, he has good ideas. And with these we've forged ahead, so that now the cooperative has almost 1000 tons of our own steel." This, she averred, "has given the cooperative the market penetration we have now."

For Pascual, the desperation of 2001 had become "an anecdote. And I've never said this to anyone," he added, "but a person learns to value many things after this. Before I had my job, I had my salary, and I didn't think about anyone else. A person doesn't value these things. I learned to value them when what happened to me happened. Today, we truly value our cooperative. We love our cooperative. That's why we've had the success we had, for all the responsibilities every one of us takes on."

The success of Los Constituyentes was replicated throughout the MNFRT, as well as the various smaller associations that took over from the MNER, as two of its main proponents, Eduardo Murúa and Diego Kravitz, bucked the 2003 electoral trend and won seats in local government. Some of the former MNER workplaces re-grouped in the Federation of Cooperatives Managed by Workers (FACTA) and the Printers Cooperatives Network. Others, as well as newly recuperated workplaces, joined organizations such as the National Federation of Work Cooperatives of Recovered Enterprises (Fenocooter) and National Federation of Worker Cooperatives (Fecootra).

For Luis Caro, there was "ever more internal growth in the cooperatives in general." While this could be put down to the fact that they were exempt from taxes and the economy had grown, it was not the main reason, he said. "Rather it has more to do with being a product of the workers' organization. The economic improvement is important, of course, but in Argentina, you have to take this improvement with a grain of salt. It exists in certain sectors but not for the population in general."

Aside from the tax structure, the economic upturn and the workers' own efforts and determination, another basic reason underlay their success. This was the lack of what Esteban Magnani has called "owner cost." The owner of a firm needs to pay his staff and reap a profit on top of expenditures; the cooperative members need only pay themselves, making what would be unviable to a business owner perfectly viable to them. It has also been remarkable the way plant workers, in many instances, have been easily able to carry out the functions of managers as well as marketing and sales departments, white collar jobs that have traditionally paid substantially more than assembly line labour.

"In order to maintain production, the capitalist always needs controllers making sure that the worker is producing well," said Caro. "In this case, since the workers participate in the profits, they concern themselves every day with improving production to obtain the maximum, to assist the client, increase the number of clients, innovate in production and cut costs."

This tendency among the self-managed cooperatives also underlines why nationalization would neither generate the same effect nor truly empower these groups of workers. Were the state to agree to financially support the enterprise regardless of its feasibility, the search for efficiencies and the creativity of worker members would be completely unnecessary, if not undesirable. So, as Caro said, the MNFRT cooperatives believe that they "are generating another kind of system, of working, of producing, of sharing the wealth."

Indeed, even as the economy in Argentina improved, private companies continued to go bankrupt and their workers continued to take them over. Economic policy may offer one rationalization for such business failures, but it has been apparent that human error — the errors of their owners — is another. It has been into these interstices that the movement seeps, and will continue to do so. Several workers interviewed mentioned that when a second or third generation of owners took over, they frequently showed little interest in the company itself, managed it poorly and encountered problems. Others, expecting a better return, preferred to invest profits in the financial markets — or even abroad — rather than in the enterprise itself. In some cases, demand seemed high while owners claimed they were going broke. At Lavalan, for example, many workers were fired, then immediately rehired as casual labour. Matilde Adorno, a Brukman worker, also described how, prior to the owners abandoning the factory, employees were turning out hundreds of suits every day at the same time as their wages were constantly cut back. At Los Constituyentes, the previous owner had maintained three separate sets of books and used eighty different bank accounts.

Because of their own achievements, every worker interviewed emphasized that workers facing the sack because their workplace was shutting down now had another option to consider beyond severance pay or unemployment. "Yesterday I was with a group of workers who went to visit a recuperated cooperative," said Caro. "They heard that their factory is closing and they called me. Last week there was another, and last month another. Today, we can say that we are an alternative if a factory has to close down." In fact, for City University of New York's Peter Ranis, Argentina's worker cooperative movement raises questions regarding not only the country's political economy "but redounds globally, everywhere workers are confronted with outsourcing, downsizing and arbitrary decisions by the owners and managers of capitalist enterprises."

Still very much an incipient movement, only time will tell whether it will thrive and expand, remain static or — given the many challenges it faces — fall apart. The recuperated workplaces continue to function within the logic of global capitalism, using often old machinery and, in all but a few cases, at production levels still below those of their founders' best years. While organizations like Buenos Aires-based La Base, where Magnani now works, provide useful, flexible micro-loans to many recuperated workplaces, in general they have little access to capital in the form of loans and subsidies. The MNFRT itself lacks the time and money to maintain consolidating lines of communication, such as a monthly bulletin or even an actualized website, among members.

"While some (cooperatives) are open to the community, or try to be," said Natalia Polti, "the rhythms of work continue to be the rhythm of capital. They are cooperatives, but they are inserted in the capitalist marketplace with schedules that are marked by this marketplace. They have to be profitable, and if they are not, it makes no sense."

Nonetheless, certain aspects of the MNFRT leave a strong impression that it will continue to grow and evolve. One is its autonomy, its ability, as Pedro Casaldaliga suggested to the Landless Rural Workers Movement, "to walk on its own two feet." A series of factors have led not only the MNFRT but the cooperative movement in general to harbour a profound desire for independence. For Magnani, in fact, it is a sentiment at times closer to wariness or distrust. Cooperative workers have been exploited by predatory employers, let down sharply by their trade unions and largely ignored by the government. While small political parties of the left may have championed their crucial role in a productive society and their rights, they have been unable to understand the workers' need to assume the reins of productive power and decision-making themselves. An unfortunate inclination for sectarianism, which played havoc among the *piqueteros*, for example, also aggravated the cooperatives' tendency to shy away from ideology. From their very beginning, said Magnani, "a major degree of autonomy is already encrypted in the genetics of the recuperated factory."

Some cooperatives have also encountered greed and dishonesty from within. Both the Hospital Israelita and the Navales Unidos shipyard have dealt with administrative councils set on personal agendas. Sprawled along the muddy banks of the Riachuelo River across from Buenos Aires, Navales Unidos spent six months working on a major ship repair in 2003. "We worked twelve hours a day, the height of summer, taking home 50 to 100 pesos a week," recalled cooperative secretary José Alberto Aquino. Expecting their big pay-off once the project was finished, suddenly "the numbers didn't add up," he said. "The administrative council we had then, thinking they could get away with it, dared to do what they had no right to do," making a deal with the ship owner behind the workers' backs and absconding with some $50,000. When asked why the workers did not become demoralized after such a terrible setback, he answered, "Because we knew we could do things well. We were convinced that things could change and with an honest administrative council, we would progress. There was a lot of work and we could change this retrograde mentality." Four years had proven the truth of José Alberto's prediction, so that for Caro, the movement's autonomy stems from each cooperative's economic achievements. "They don't depend on anyone," he said. "The less dependent, the better for the workers."

At the same time, links of solidarity among the cooperatives act as powerful forces for building strength and a sense of identity. They all contribute to the growth of new cooperatives, maintaining so-called solidarity funds with their earnings to help newly recuperated and struggling enterprises get on their feet. They also offer advice and go on protest marches in support of those factories having problems with former owners and the courts. Hospital Israelita offers discount medical insurance to other MNFRT members, while the December 19 Cooperative at the former Brukman factory donates suits that can be raffled off to collect money. Whenever there is a cultural event at one of the workplaces, other cooperatives send representatives, when feasible, to set up stands showing off their products. As Diana George pointed out, "One does indeed feel part of a movement. You know when you realize it? When a cooperative has problems, with expropriation, or with an eviction, and you think, these people are going through what we might have had to go through six years ago. So, many of the *compañeros* go out on marches to support these cooperatives."

As Caro put it, "The fellow in the first recuperated factory is thinking about how to help more *compañeros*. The fellow in the latest recuperated factory is calling me to go see other *compañeros*. That is the relationship of solidarity that exists."

This has meant that, like the urban poor in the Indian Alliance, cooperative members identify with their peers rather than political parties or governors, unlocking the possibility of creating a new consciousness, a space from which a completely different interpretation of the relations between capital and labour can develop. This identification is built on similar experiences, backgrounds and definitions of what is needed to maintain sources of productive employment. By framing the solution to joblessness and exploitation in their own terms, the members of the MNFRT are — in the words of Julio Rebón — "disobeying unemployment" and have thus become empowered as individuals and as social beings.

Several years ago, the Museum of Modern Art in New York put on an exhibition of works by Russian artist Alexander Rodchenko. For me, the most evocative items on display were candy wrappers; tiny, insignificant and disposable, they had been designed by the candy factory workers themselves using graphics by Rodchenko and lines of poetry from the great Russian poet, Vladimir Mayakovski. By then, these bits of paper were all that was left of those workers' creative spirit and optimism. And of the factory councils and democratic ideals of the early years of the Russian Revolution, there may be even less. Yet while they symbolized at least one poignant facet of working-class liberation and management of the means of production, their survival paralleled the aspiration among workers today for freedom from the profit logic of capitalism and all that it implies.

As we search for signs of the realization of such aspirations, it isn't difficult to become discouraged. As Boaventura de Souza Santos and César Rodríguez Garavito pointed out in the introduction to *Another Production Is Possible*, "Given the endurance of neoliberal capitalism, it is easy to take desperate or cynical stances regarding any alternative. For impatient minds, such pessimism comes easily, and the absence of any radical break with the status quo generates scepticism about any gradually implemented or local alternative."

However, in Argentina's recuperated enterprises we do find an emancipating challenge, from below, to the strictures of modern-day capitalism and the poverty it sows. If thousands of workers can run their workplace, whether it be a factory, a hospital, a supermarket or a school, without a boss, one cannot help but ask why society needs bosses at all. "When you think about it," said Hospital Israelita's Eleonora Berton, "these businessmen, these owners, make their investments and do their managing, but who does the work are the people who are there, day after day. A place can function without its owners, but never without its workers."

The recession provoked by a financial crisis in the most powerful economy of them all has, therefore, been a litmus test of just how feasible and inspiring the factory recuperation movement might be. By the middle of 2008, national economies around the world were suffering the effects of the profound downturn in the United States, one characterized by oceans of debt, home foreclosures and lay-offs. In Argentina as well, economic growth stalled and flattened. At the same time, however, a new wave of factory takeovers began. In May 2009, Caro was once again fielding phone calls from workers on the floors of bankrupt companies. Sitting in a vacant office in the Vieyetes ice cream cooperative one darkening evening, the South American winter approaching, he had just that afternoon been to talk to forty workers at Famel S.A. A company making oil, air and water filters for heavy machinery, its elderly owners had left a grandson in charge, he explained; "it hasn't been doing very well and he hasn't been paying the workers."

He went on: "There are six or seven more enterprises entering into conflicts at the moment." These included Audiovic, a factory that made televisions and video cassette players in Tierra del Fuego, a paper plant in San Luis and an automotive glass factory in Cordoba. The workers of a local auto parts plant that had declared bankruptcy two weeks earlier had just been authorized to reactivate production, after the police had attempted to evict them. Indeed, in the first half of 2009, newspapers reported on twenty firms taken over by their workers.

This new wave was already proving itself to be somewhat distinct from the previous iteration. Both inside and outside the MNFRT, the process of forming cooperatives, claiming abandoned workplaces and gearing up production under worker management was occurring far more quickly and with less confrontation than in 2001 and 2002. "It is different now because there is an example," said Magnani. "For that reason, (the workers) don't wait as long to re-start production, because they see that once they do, the situation is much better. First of all they can eat, secondly, they show the rest of society that they can make a go of it, and thirdly, it generates a social legitimacy that makes it much more difficult to evict them."

By the end of 2010, Argentina's congress was finally debating changes to the nation's bankruptcy law as well. Strongly promoted by the MNFRT, these included provisions allowing workers to continue production even as owners applied for creditor protection and set the value of their stake at 100 percent of monies and benefits owed to them, instead of the current 50 percent. According to the newspaper *Pagina 12*, there were some 3000 shuttered workplaces throughout the country, "many of which could re-emerge in the hands of their former workers if they had the facilities put forth in the initiative under study."

Nonetheless, lower demand also affected the older workplace cooperatives. At Los Constituyentes, orders — and production — fell by half in 2009. According to Alejandro Coronel, about 70 percent of its clients came from the construction, automotive and agricultural machinery sectors, those suffering the most from the economic downturn. "In most companies in this situation," he said, "they reduce their size and fire staff. But we are against that. We came at it with a different idea. We decided not to fire anyone but to lower our salaries in order to maintain a return."

In a general assembly, he explained, the workers decided to take home 30 percent less than what they had been earning and to lower their prices slightly. As a result, they found that clients were gradually starting to approach them again. "We're not making huge amounts of money," he said, "but no one can take away our salaries. We can maintain ourselves, our families and the factory, and that means we're doing well. All the rest is secondary."

As remarkable perhaps as the upbeat atmosphere at the cooperative were its plans for the future, ideas for projects that went beyond production issues.

Ever since its founding, Los Constituyentes, like many others, had fostered close ties with the surrounding community. In many cases, those ties were reflective of the support and solidarity they had received from their neighbourhoods while still unsure whether they would be allowed to proceed or not. Andrés Ruggeri of the Centre for the Documentation of Recuperated Businesses has described this opening of the factory to the community as the most important of "a series of concrete social innovations in which the self-management of production and the formation of solidarity networks… have been put into play." These social innovations, he adds, "tend not to be technological innovations but, rather, different social mechanisms used to operate a business that continues to function within the context of a market."

According to Alejandro, Los Constituyentes had received many visits from local school groups over the previous years. Occasionally warned by parents that they would be entering the lair of troublemakers or "*piqueteros*," as Alejandro explained it, they always left with an image at variance with what they had been expecting. "They're quite surprised," he said, "and this matters a lot to me."

The cooperative was also a subject of research for university students and academics, he added, yet he often found that their conclusions did not fairly represent what was really going on there. Considering both issues, cooperative members had therefore decided to establish an information and training centre on the office's vacant upper floor. Its first priority would be raising the skills of other workers, beginning with the factory itself. Eventually, however, the plan was "to open it up to the community, so that people see this model," said Alejandro, "this model of recuperating and managing the workplace."

For him personally, he emphasized, and for the entire movement, "the most important thing that can happen to the factory takeover movement is that it carries on repeating itself. That people realize that they can do it, that the workers can take over a factory and do it well. For the worker to become a person who isn't alienated from the idea that they can win this, they have to have it seen it somewhere."

The idea, as Alejandro outlined it, was to open up a space where workers could chat in an informal way about what was happening there and at scores of other workplaces, using this as a basis for discussion and debate. It would, therefore, be distinct from the cultural spaces some members of popular assemblies had tried to set up in recuperated workplaces, such as the Nueva Esperanza breadstick factory.

The Constituyentes project, rather, would respond to what its workers believed to be of value to them and others like them. "I believe we should have a place where we do our own research," said Alejandro, "because for us too it is a new model, just like it is for everybody. We've been learning as we go along. So it is really important to document all these experiences and learn from ourselves so that the recuperated factories, the cooperatives that are still being born, can avoid some of the obstacles and errors." What's more, its activities and exchange of knowledge would reflect the democratic decision-making that characterizes the cooperative itself, so that, in the words of Alejandro, "it be us who are talking about the factory."

This desire to take charge of their own story signals further the empowering potential of the process of recuperating the workplace itself and is reminiscent of the creativity and decision-making powers of the earliest examples of the factory council. Growing at its own pace, concentrating in its still early years on short and medium term objectives, the takeover movement nonetheless challenges not only neo-liberal economic policies but also the traditional politics of opposition to it. For Ranis, these "islands of worker autonomy and responsibility" offer "the promise of new forms of worker control over the productive process, worker political empowerment and a potential revision of traditional relations between capital and labor." And as they extend the narrative of their achievements into surrounding and broader communities, along with what Ranis calls their "critique of the neo-liberal business-as-usual ethos," the workplace cooperatives also offer an undeniable source of inspiration to civil society in Argentina.

Indeed, as Santos and Rodríguez Garavito have suggested, "in many cases, gradual changes and small-scale alternatives open doors for gradual structural transformations. The seeds of large-scale emancipation can be sown in these small fields of opportunity."

In the end, each recuperated workplace, within all of the organizations that make up the factory recuperation movement, is the seed of a new and different future. "People ask me, 'where's the ceiling?'" said Alejandro Coronel. "Me, I don't see the ceiling. We can do a ton of things." Just like the movements previously described, the National Movement of Factories Recovered by Workers is yet another indication of how disadvantaged members of society are finding ways to transform vulnerability into strength and poverty into the success story of a better life. Their dramatic counterposing of the privileges of the business class against the rights of a working class threatened by unemployment and poverty attacks the very logic that lies at the heart of the system. The worker-managed enterprises of Argentina thus offer a glimpse into a future where the creative energy and spirit of the working class is liberated and the exploitation of the majority for the profit of a minority a thing of the past.

Conclusion

No Turning Back

This book explores the way grassroots social movements confront the abject conditions in which their members live — or would undoubtedly live if they were to accept the narrow horizons of unemployment and landlessness — with answers both sustainable and profound. Their independence, democratic decision-making and creativity play important roles in their ability to do so. But at heart, it is their recognition of, and struggle for, their basic rights that inform those sustainable solutions.

Yet the principle question remains: can their success in challenging and changing their destinies be replicated elsewhere? It is my belief that as the system persists in denying the right of the poor to human wellbeing, not only, but particularly, in the developing world, grassroots social movements will, in turn, keep forming and fighting for that right. This is a system that sows resistance to itself, littering the way forward with obstacles, bureaucracy, doublespeak and greed — or just plain indifference. But even in the face of repression, the spirit embodied in each of the millions of people who feel they have no other recourse but to struggle against it is shared by millions more.

The existence of other social movements, with differing strategies yet similarly remarkable achievements to their collective credit, support this hopeful, rather than wishful, claim. Among them is the Self-Employed Women's Association, or SEWA, based in Ahmedabad, capital of the Indian state of Gujarat. In 1971, Ela Bhatt was working in the legal department of the Textile Labour Association, a trade union co-founded in 1920 by Mahatma Ghandi. One day a group of women cart pullers who worked in the local market came in with their contractor, wondering if the TLA could do anything about finding housing for them. Ela Bhatt had already checked into complaints from tailors who worked at home regarding their exploitation by contractors and had carried out a larger survey of similarly self-employed women unprotected by either unions or government. Accompanying her visitors to the market, she met other women who earned small and erratic wages for the gruelling task of pulling or bearing heavy bundles of clothing between the wholesale and retail markets. At a public meeting in a city park, a hundred women showed up and suggested they too form a union, so that by December 1971, the Self-Employed Women's Association had formed within the TLA. It was officially registered as a trade union the following year.

Interestingly, less than a decade later, SEWA left the TLA thanks to at least two internal contradictions. One was the TLA's unwillingness to take a clear anti-discriminatory position against the violence brought against its Harijan members during riots stemming from the demand by higher caste medical students to end the government-mandated process of reserving places for Harijan and other so-called scheduled castes or scheduled tribes. The second, however, had to do with the almost natural conflict to be found within a traditional trade union representing formally recognized workers and the even more exploitable informal workers with whom they must increasingly compete.

Today, with more than 900,000 members across India, SEWA not only runs its own micro-bank, with 200,000 clients, and works on housing issues, it also advocates for better wages for all kinds of piecework done at home. These tasks include anything from making incense sticks, to rolling cigarettes, to sewing and embroidery. Aside from those self-employed inside the home, SEWA also represents women who collect gum and make salt, helping them bypass agents to sell directly into a larger marketplace. For Ela Bhatt, the entrepreneurship and initiative taken by the poor "develops all aspects of the person — the social, the economic and the political. There is room for all kinds of development," she wrote, "and it is crucial to nurture the entrepreneurship the poor show in their fight to survive."

As manufacturers continued to drum down wages, pitting informal labourers ever more against each other and against organized workforces, SEWA joined up fifteen years ago with HomeNet and StreetNet, agglomerations of all-but-invisible, informal workers in twenty-five countries all over the world. As parts of Women in Informal Employment, Globalizing and Organizing, or WEIGO, these two umbrella networks were instrumental in the International Labour Organization's adoption of a Convention on Home Work in 1996. The individual grassroots organizations, meanwhile, continue to lobby their national governments to implement and enforce the standards and protections set down within the ILO Convention.

In Chapters Three and Four, we looked at the efforts of forest dwellers in Southeast Asia to take on the right to manage their forest habitats and earn a living at the same time. In Nepal as well, millions of forest dwellers unified within the Federation of Community Forest Users, or FECOFUN, have organized to protect not only the forest but their right to manage its resources. So-called forest user groups were originally set up in 1993, shortly after widespread protests forced the Nepali monarchy to accept constitutional reforms and establish a parliament. Its passing of the Forest Act assigned rights over forested land to thousands of small rural communities. Yet this official recognition of their rights did not mean that forests were no longer in danger of destruction from corporations, the state and new settlements, particularly in the populous Terai region.

In 1995, several forest-user groups decided to form a federation that has, over the years, united more than 11,000 communities throughout almost all of Nepal's 75 districts. Fighting on two fronts, it relies on mass rallies, advocacy and negotiation to deepen and broaden the rights of its members. Involved in a constant struggle to stop attempts to curtail community rights and misappropriate land and timber, FECOFUN also works with members to conserve and manage community forests. It has developed various ways to market forest products, and communities are now using the profits from these to build schools, improve roads, set up micro-finance schemes and promote literacy. What's more, according to Hemant Ojha and Netra Timsina, "In recent years, FECOFUN's contribution has gone beyond the forestry sector and has played an important role in political movements against feudal monarchy towards establishing (democracy) in the country."

Resistance to the rampant exploitation of resources that only serves to increase poverty was also the main motivation in the formation of the Samacha Khon Chon, or Assembly of the Poor, in Thailand. It was founded in 1995, spurred to life by villagers whose livelihoods had been destroyed by the construction of the Pak Mun dam, a project on which the World Bank spent $24 million. Eventually acknowledged by the World Commission on Dams to have no economic justification in terms of the amount of hydro-electric power generated, it nonetheless ruined the ecology of the Mun River. Fifty species of rapid dependent fish disappeared, as the fish ladders devised by World Bank experts proved to be completely useless, while over a hundred more declined in stock by between 60 and 80 percent.

Initial protest marches and occupations won some financial compensation for the Pak Mun villagers committee, and this small victory led to the broadening of the mobilization into a much larger movement. The Assembly of the Poor soon evolved into a vibrant network of nineteen groups "of struggling poor and urban people," as they themselves put it, united by their common grievances. Its founding document vowed "to build the power and cooperation of the poor at the local, national and international levels to convince the public that states must manage resources in ways that ensure equity and fairness for all people, free rights, and popular participation and self-determination."

The Assembly is in many ways a network of grievances, its members' demands reflecting the havoc Thailand's post-war push for industrialization has wreaked on their lives. It includes villagers trying to stop the functioning or construction of five dams, rural workers seeking land reform and a ban on pesticides, slum dwellers from Bangkok and Chang Mai demanding proper housing and peasants forced out of areas they had long occupied when the government retroactively designated their land forest reserves. Replanted with eucalyptus for the pulp-and-paper industry, the effects of the latter have been as catastrophic as the damming of rivers. In some areas, plantations are irrigated with local pulp mill effluent, which kills other vegetation and contaminates the water table.

Those joining the Assembly do so with the understanding that they will remain until every problem is dealt with, becoming "hubs in a network of communication, negotiation and compromise between the community organizations and the network as a whole," wrote Bruce Missingham in *The Assembly of the Poor in Thailand*. This solidarity underlines the realization that, while their nation's development path affects different communities in different ways, it is based on a central precept — that of fortifying capitalist development — and this is targeted in all of their protests.

At the same time, this movement has encouraged democratic and decentralized decision-making among its various groups. According to Missingham, "the Assembly endeavours to retain the original form in which representatives of villages and NGOs come together to share knowledge and experiences, make decisions collectively and democratically, and devise collective responses and strategies." This is done through meetings of *pho kou yai*, elected representatives who meet regularly and bring home issues to be discussed by the different groups, and from there, each village.

Years of direct action, marches and lengthy occupations of the public space in Bangkok have forced successive governments to meet many of their demands. Yet as Missingham pointed out, "successive governments have appeased Assembly protests with public promises to address their problems and petitions, and then tied them up in lengthy bureaucratic committee processes which announce symbolic decisions but result in little action." From the 1997 economic crisis to the 2006 military coup that ousted the populist government of Thaksin Shinawatra, the past decade and a half have brought great changes to Thailand's political, social and economic contexts and, for Missingham, "the Assembly has largely failed to find new or innovative strategies within those rapidly changing conditions."

The Assembly of the Poor, therefore, is confronting major challenges, and while it does so from a position of demoralization and frustration, it may well learn from its history and recover momentum. It has happened to other social movements in the past. And as Missingham has also pointed out, many in the Mun River Villagers Committee, "say that fighting against the Pak Mun dam is their *kam*, their destiny in life." The demands of all the Assembly members and their solutions to economic and environmental destruction remain powerful potential measures to deal with Thailand's crushing poverty burden and its degraded environment.

In spite of their setbacks, the resilience of the poor is truly remarkable. Scott Beck and Ken Mijeski have found this even among members of the Confederation of Indigenous Nationalities in Ecuador, who succeeded in bringing the Rafael Correa government to the table to revise a new mining law. "The indigenous movement, particularly at the bases, is very resilient," said Beck, "because it's based around indigenous communities in the rural areas that still have a communitarian ideal. It still makes sense to them to make decisions together and do things together, and to feel part of something larger." While it does not have the mobilization power it once had, he added, "there's still something there."

And to these movements I believe it is fair to add the plethora of smaller organizations and community groups that swell the flow of struggle against global poverty with hundreds if not thousands of laudable yet all-but-imperceptible initiatives for change. In South Africa, the Abahlali baseMdojono has several thousand members living in the slums of Durban and Pietermaritzburg. For years they have born the brunt of violent evictions, beatings and even killings at the hands of the African National Congress government, yet they have never lost their sense of combativeness and independence. In 2009, local housing authorities finally agreed to recognize tenure rights and build new housing in three Abahlali settlements and upgrade fourteen others. The organization scored another victory when its court challenge of the Kwazulu-Natal Slums Act — which would not only have allowed municipalities to evict the poor from public lands but impel landlords to force them off private lands as well — was successful.

In Somaliland, a group of young men, their childhoods devastated by the Somalian Civil War, came together in the early 1990s to form the General Assistance and Volunteer Organization (GAVO) in the port city of Berbera. Wanting to deal with some of city's most glaring social needs, GAVO's initial focus was on psychiatric patients suffering from war-induced trauma living at the local hospital. They began by simply taking care of some of their personal needs, then went on to seek donations from city merchants and to use popular theatre to educate people about, and erase the stigma from, mental illness. Eventually, international organizations began to see GAVO as a valuable contact point, with a strong local resource base and a prominent reputation in its community. Oxfam, for example, offered small amounts of funding but concentrated on helping members improve management skills through courses, travel to similar communities and advice from development economists. UN-HABITAT approached it with a plan to rebuild the port's central market, which led GAVO to set up a consultation process whereby religious leaders, vendors and purchasers were able to have a say in the project through a series of open discussions and dialogue. The organization has since taken on the entire management of the local hospital and launched a program for street children. More importantly, it has spread to other parts of the country, promoting participatory governance and helping to broaden the impoverished nation's democratization process.

On the other side of the African continent, in Senegal, a somewhat similar process led to the formation in 1994 of CADEL — the Collective for the Support of Local Development — in Sebikhotane. "We were a group who had the luck to go to school," said Eliman Kane, "who were educated up to a certain level, but who came from agriculture, particularly market gardening." Their initial aspiration was to modernize peasant farming and "work directly with exporters, who could sell our produce abroad for ten or twenty times more than what we were getting," he added. "But they said we couldn't do that. So we had to find out how to access these systems, and that is when we began to organize."

CADEL now has several hundred members in various internal groupings, for farmers, for women and children, for artisans and so on. It also has a dozen volunteers, both men and women, who work as *animateurs* and who link the elected CADEL steering committee to its membership. According to its treasurer, Mame Issa Poeye, they look at a particular problem, make a diagnosis of it and decide what they can do to resolve it, then look for partners to help them out. On the issue of poverty, for example, they decided to start up a savings and micro-credit scheme, getting help from an already existing network of such *caisses* already running in Senegal. For health care, they decided to establish a health mutual, Jappo Wer (meaning Union for Health) that today has almost 600 members. They set up literacy programs for women, school nutrition programs for children and even a radio station, supported by an internet café, that broadcasts useful information to the community.

Although the people of the region around Sebikhotane still suffer many basic difficulties, participation in CADEL is slowly having an effect in bettering the lives of its members. "Perhaps," said Mame, "through managing to bring about some local development, we can eventually achieve national development."

Further north, near Louga, years of drought sparked the formation of the Union of Peasant Groups of Mehknes in 1985. "The land had become degraded after years of planting peanuts," said Ndiakate Fall, secretary of the UGPM, "and above all from the drying out of the environment." Union members began to consult their elders in a search for solutions that might bring their farms back to life. They began a campaign that eventually saw tens of thousands of trees, including baobabs, juniper and fruit trees, planted around small plots. Any farmer joining the union, which has grown from five villages to eighty-two and has some 5000 members, is obliged to plant trees. They also went back to growing typical food crops such as millet and cowpeas and using organic fertilizers instead of chemical ones.

Utilizing strategically chosen international partners, other UGPM campaigns have resulted in micro-credit schemes, seed banks and free seeds from the government, community wells, solar panels for electricity and efforts to help families better manage consumption, reducing the periods of *soudure* — the time between food running out and the next harvest. This, for example, the organization did by taking on the long-cherished custom of celebrating religious and family holidays with feasts families could ill afford, opening a dialogue with the people and their religious leaders about it.

While not every organization approaches poverty from a position of demanding certain rights, they do illustrate the fact that partnerships and community decision-making are extremely effective routes to resource distribution. They are proof that development efforts from afar are most successful when they are accompanied by long-term relationships, as David Satterthwaite pointed out in Chapter Five, and when it is the aid recipients themselves who drive the multitude of projects that go on every day in hundreds of poor countries around the world.

So while the importance of autonomy — of a movement's ability to not only walk on its own feet but also think with its own head — has been demonstrated numerous times by the organized poor, this raises another salient issue: what is the role of activists and advocates in more affluent nations, of progressive political parties, NGOs and labour unions?

I believe this role must be one of solidarity and partnership, of building equiponderant relationships. In fact, together with that of organized social activity, we are already seeing the concomitant growth of international networks across borders and hemispheres, an indispensable buttress against international alliances between national governments and globalized capital. Fertile ground for the exchange of ideas, experiences, strategies and the ongoing narratives of progress, the global summits set up and attended by these organizations continue to proliferate, attracting increasing numbers of activists every year.

Solidarity with grassroots movements, moreover, can often push the boundaries of NGOs based in wealthy nations beyond education and advocacy campaigns as they endorse human rights and more radical forms of struggle. The international research and advocacy platform for women who work in the informal economy, WIEGO, may be based at Harvard University's Hauser Center for Nonprofit Organizations, but its steering committee includes representatives of grassroots organizations and its agendas are fixed after annual meetings they attend. "This innovative arrangement," wrote Srilatha Batliwala, "of separating the grassroots organizing entity and the international advocacy entity, but ensuring the latter is accountable to the former, has enabled… WIEGO to have immense impact on the public policy environment in a relatively short space of time."

Once simply an environmental organization, Berkeley, Ca.-based International Rivers also works with people whose rights are swallowed up by their national governments' determination to harness the flow of rivers and offer large, often multinational firms the fiscal lure of cheap energy. It supports the struggles of the Movement of People Affected by Dams in Brazil, the Assembly of the Poor in Thailand, and grassroots organizations, grassroots movements and NGOs in other Latin American countries and in Cambodia and India, where the combative Narmada Bachao Andolan continues to mobilize against dam projects scheduled for the Narmada River.

Yet as members of the internationals into which they link themselves, these movements have achieved more than policy change. They have also changed the way their members see themselves at international forums. As Batliwala has pointed out, "they do not ask to be heard because they are down-trodden and deserving, or out of some moral obligation on the part of the powerful. They see themselves as populations playing vital roles in both macro- and micro-economic contexts.... This is a subtle but important psychological shift for both themselves and the institutions they seek to engage — it is an 'empowering mindset,' demanding to be taken seriously rather than pleading for a place at the table."

While the existence of these and other international umbrella networks augur much potential growth of and within grassroots social movements of the Global South, the relevance to poor and indigenous people in Canada of this 'empowering mindset' is compelling. Much of what the poor have achieved in the developing world can be inspiring and instructive here as well. Why are people on social assistance not allowed to be more entrepreneurial and innovative in seeking solutions to their poverty instead of being punished by provincial bureaucracy by having benefits clawed back when they earn extra money? Such regulatory condescension obliterates any incentive to take the first steps to something that might improve their future wellbeing in the long term, but for which there is as yet no guarantee. What's more, could the residents of social housing projects, which are often inadequately maintained, not organize and manage them themselves? And with housing crises in so many First Nations communities, could their own designs and criteria for the construction of homes offer a way out of this impasse — and the standardized, inadequate structures in which they now live? In other words, if bringing the voices, the priorities and the strategies of the poor into the debate can help eradicate poverty in developing nations, there seems no reason why it cannot in rich nations as well.

In the end, their achievements shine a bright light on their still insufficiently recognized ability and desire to collectively work for equality and justice — and on the road forward. As the current system in which we live continues to enable environmental ruin, war and poverty, grassroots social movements of the poor may well be the key to the collective building of an entirely new one.

Notes

INTRODUCTION

Page 2– Mark Swilling, (2005) "Hear the Forest Grow: An SDI Case Study — Africa," report commissioned by the SDI.

Page 3– India childhood malnutrition — see the National Family Health Survey website at <nfhsindia.org>.

Page 3– "piecemeal improvements…" — At the tenth anniversary summit in September 2010 of the document's signing, many contradictions in the progress of the MDGs were highlighted, from the fact that while the percentage of the population living on less than $1.25 a day went down in Ethiopia (from 60 to 16 percent), it shot up in the Democratic Republic of Congo, from 49 to 77 percent. Primary school enrolment in African countries was up, but investment in education was not. What's more, even if all of the MDGs are met, a billion people will still live in poverty.

Page 5– Peter Ranis (2005) "Argentina's Worker Occupied Factories and Enterprises," *Socialism and Democracy*, 19, 3.

Page 6– Anthony Oliver-Smith (2001) "Displacement, Resistance and the Critique of Development: From the Grassroots to the Global," report prepared for ESCOR R7644 and the Research Programme on Development Induced Displacement and Resettlement, Refugee Centre, University of Oxford. See also *Defying Displacement, Grassroots Resistance and the Critique of Development* (2010) University of Texas Press, Austin.

Page 6– Born in Mannville, Alberta, in 1922, the influential sociologist Erving Goffman elaborated his theory of how conceptual frames structure an individual's experience in his 1974 book, *Frame Analysis: An Essay on the Organization of Experience*. This concept has been subsequently developed in social movement theory and policy studies.

Page 8– Reduced Emissions from Deforestation and Forest Degradation is a method supported by the international community, including sovereign nations and the World Bank, that uses market incentives to encourage rain forest nations to reduce the emission of greenhouse gasses through deforestation. It was first developed at the United Nations-sponsored Conference of Parties in Montreal in 2005.

Page 8– Srilatha Batliwala (2002) "Grassroots Movements as Transnational Actors: Implications for Global Civil Society," *Voluntas*, 13, 4.

Page 12– Tony Benn, from an interview with *The Guardian*, May 31, 2007.

CHAPTER 1

Page 18– The MLST made headlines in May 2006 when its members trashed the lobby of the Chamber of Deputies during a protest march in Brasilia.

Page 18– "...its own university" — Located in Guararema, São Paulo, it is called the Florestan Fernandes National School.

Page 19– INCRA stands for the National Institute for Colonization and Agrarian Reform.

Page 20– Jan Rocha and Sue Branford (2002) *Cutting the Wire: The Story of the Landless Movement in Brazil*, Latin America Bureau, London.

Page 20– Horácio Martins de Carvalho (2006) "The Emancipation of the Movement of Landless Rural Workers within the Continual Movement of Social Emancipation," in *Another Production Is Possible: Beyond the Capitalist Canon*, Boaventura de Souza Santos, ed. Verso, London.

Page 21– "...protests from the base." — from Rocha and Branford, *Cutting the Wire*. In *Stuffed and Starved: The Hidden Battle for the World Food System* (2007) Portobello Books, London, Raj Patel came to similar conclusions: "The MST isn't infallible. No movement is. What makes this movement interesting is that, because it takes its democracy seriously, and takes seriously the thinking that such commitment involves, it is able to recover from its mistakes."

Page 22– Manuel Domingos (2003) *Land Reform in Brazil*, Backgrounder for Land Action Research Network, Oakland, CA.

Page 24– "...basic government food rations" — A larger and more prevalent program, still in use in Brazil, is called the Bolsa Familia – or "family pocketbook." It provides small amounts of money to families who keep their children in school and is distributed to an estimated 13 million Brazilians.

Page 24– I am indebted to ornithologist Arthur Grosset for helping me identify the English names for these birds.

Page 25– "...for lectures and *misticas*." — According to Rocha and Branford, *Cutting the Wire*, the *mistica* is probably based on songs and rituals from the early occupations "when progressive Catholic priests had encouraged the families in the camps to reshape Catholic rites to make them relevant to their own struggle and culture." One MST member they interviewed described them as "an injection of vitality which gives us determination and daring so that we can overcome pessimism and push ahead with our project for including the excluded in the liberation of the Brazilian people."

Page 30– Brenda Baletti, Tamara Johnson and Wendy Wolford (2008) "Late Mobilization: Transnational Peasant Networks and Grassroots Organizing in Brazil and South Africa," in *Transnational Agrarian Movements Confronting Globalization*, S. Borras, ed., Wiley Blackwell, Hoboken, NJ.

Page 30– "...decide their own destiny." — From Rocha and Branford, *Cutting the Wire*.

CHAPTER 2

Page 32– "...afraid of us." — In fact, the mainstream media in Brazil remains stubbornly inimical to the MST and the activities of its members in taking land. A review of 300 articles about the MST in Brazil's four largest-circulation dailies by a human rights group called Rede Social found only eight that were neutral or partly positive. Nonetheless, Globo Network did produce a soap opera with a subplot involving the taking of land by landless rural workers, although one of them, a young woman, turned out to be the long-lost daughter of a millionaire.

Page 33– The Araguaia guerrilla, instigated by the Communist Party of Brazil in the late 1960s in opposition to the military government, was snuffed out by the armed forces between 1972 and 1974.

Page 34– Agent Orange — from Rocha and Branford, *Cutting the Wire.*

Page 34– "…a boyhood friend…" — Gabriel A. Ondetti has described Rainha as "the biggest exception to the rule of non-personalistic leadership within the MST. Although the regional MST was formally organized collectively, he was quite clearly the central figure by virtue of his intelligence and personal charisma." Rainha left the MST in 2007; at issue was his refusal to stay out of party politics and preference for a strategy whereby landless peasants negotiate with landowners before occupying roadsides to demand the expropriation of the estate. He has formed a new organization and claims to have 6000 members.

Page 36– "…even more profits" — According to Philip McMichael, "artificially cheapened food surplus exports from the North are based on subsidies that can reduce prices by as much as 57 percent below actual costs and have a devastating effect on small farmers in the Global South."

Page 36– "…dismantle their farm marketing boards." —— Mexico is an excellent example of this. The Archer Daniels Midland-Grupo Maseca (Gruma) consortium controls 73 percent of Mexico's corn flour market, and Minsa and Cargill most of the rest. Also, see <www.oaklandinstitute.org/pdfs/fasr.pdf> (on agribusiness and dumping)

Page 37– Saturnino Borras (2008). "La Vía Campesina and Its Global Campaign for Agrarian Reform," in *Transnational Agrarian Movements Confronting Globalization,* Wiley Blackwell, Hoboken, NJ.

Page 38– "…will take on." — The United Nation's Food and Agriculture Organization publishes a world agriculture census and puts out a selection of on-line documents. These indicate the numbers of smallholders and the totality of land they farm, yet fails to identify large estates beyond anywhere from 10 to 60 hectares. It is also missing the statistics of many low-income nations. Those from the Philippines are from Borras.

Page 38– "alarming new trend…" — See John Vidal, *The Guardian,* March 7, 2010; Julian Borger, *The Guardian,* November 22, 2008; Sue Branford, Latin America Bureau, and many others.

Page 38– Aracruz — Isabella Kenfield, (2007). *Taking on Big Cellulose: Brazilian Indigenous Communities Reclaim Their Land.* North American Congress on Latin America (NACLA). <www.mediaaccuracy.org/files/pdfs/Amazon_Cellulose.pdf>

Page 39– BNDES. Founded in 1953, BNDES is now the world's third-largest development bank, with a budget of more than US$300 billion, according to Brasil de Fato. Like the World Bank, the vast majority of its public resources are funnelled to major corporations and multinationals, including Aracruz, Votorantim and Companhia Vale do Rio Doce, owner of the Inco mine in Sudbury, Ontario. Another major recipient is JBS-Friboi, which, with 70 percent of revenues coming from its U.S. operations, is now the world's largest meat company. A watchdog group called Plataforma BNDES, made up more than thirty social movements and organizations, has been pressing for greater transparency in the Bank's allocation of loans as well as compensation for the many thousands of victims of the projects it funds.

Page 40– Sue Branford (2008) *The Landless Workers' Movement*, Latin America Bureau, London.

Page 40– Dilma Roussef made it clear before the elections that she would not tolerate land invasions by the MST.

Page 40– "unwilling to deliver meaningful land reform…" — Ariovaldo Umbelino, a professor of geography at the University of São Paulo has stated that the slower pace of expropriations of public land is common to both the Cardoso and da Silva administrations. "Lula's second term in office no longer has land reform as its objective," he told pro-government daily *Correio Braziliense*. "The targets have been dropping year after year." The MST disputes Lula's claim to have distributed land to a million families during his mandate and put the number closer to half of that. What he has done, they say, is recognize existing holdings, the majority of them in the fragile ecosystems of the Amazon.

Raj Patel, in *Stuffed and Starved*, meanwhile, finds that, "The MST does seem across the board to have produced better development outcomes than the government's own meagre land-titling programmes with better levels of long-term success."

Page 40– João Pedro Stedile (2004) "El MST y las disputas por las alternativas en Brasil," *Revista OSAL*, 13, periodical of the Latin American Council of Social Sciences, Buenos Aires.

Page 45– "…land communes" — In one of these I met Antonia Santos, a woman who had joined the occupation of empty land belonging to the municipal water authority after seeing it featured on the nightly television news. She had started growing vegetables and, with the money raised from selling her produce, bought a cow, giving away the milk to her MST neighbours. The cow had three calves, two of which she sold to improve her house.

CHAPTER 3

Page 51–Monica Di Gregorio (2006) "The Influence of Civil Society Organizations on Forest Tenure Policies in Indonesia: Networks, Strategies and Outcomes," paper presented at 11th Biannual Conference of the International Association for the Study of Common Property, Bali, Indonesia.

Page 52– "…the corruption has simply fanned out" — According to Anne Casson and Krystof Obidzinski (2007), "The boom in illegal logging can be attributed to a number of factors, including changes arising from the economic crisis, a decline in law and order, regulatory changes arising from Reformasi — a movement calling for greater democracy, reform and change — and the new decentralization laws." "New Order to Regional Autonomy: Shifting Dynamics of Illegal Logging in Kalimantan, Indonesia," in *Illegal Logging: Law Enforcement, Livelihoods and the Timber Trade*, Luca Tacconi, ed. Earthscan, London.

Page 52– "…forest loss."— J. Lawrence, N. Toyoda, and H. Helvi Lystiani (2003) *Importing Destruction*, Rainforest Action Network, San Francisco.

Page 55–Mark Dowie (2005) "Conservation Refugees," *Orion Magazine*, November/ December.

Page 56– Franklin Rothman and Pamela Oliver (1999) "From Local to Global: The Anti-Dam Movement in Southern Brazil, 1979–1992," paper presented at the American Sociological Association.

Page 57– "…interests of Brazil's power elite" — Government approval for the highly destructive Monte Belo dam on the Xingu River certainly bears this out. At a projected cost of more than $16 billion, it is slated to become the third-largest dam in the world and will disperse tens of thousands of forest and river dwellers. See amazonwatch.org

Page 58– "…in the province." — *Bangkok Post*, February 22, 2009.

Page 63– In the case of Cibaliung, Marda pointed out the drawbacks of community-based forest management, which had been offered to them. Aside from the difficulties in planting around teak, he said, agreeing to such an arrangement meant that the villagers were giving up their claim on their ancestral land.

CHAPTER 4

Page 65– Dan La Botz (2001) *Made in Indonesia: Indonesian Workers Since Suharto*, South End Press, Boston

Page 65– Andrew Rosser (2005) "Indonesia: The Politics of Inclusion," *Journal of Contemporary Asia*, 35, 1, Routledge, London.

Page 66– Placer Dome — "Government and Community Demand Placer Dome Out of Borneo," Mining Watch Canada <www.miningwatch.ca/en/government-and-community-demand-placer-dome-out-borneo>.

Page 75– This caused one of its unions, the Pasundan Peasants' Union, to drop out. It had also been long affiliated with an NGO called the Consortium for Agrarian Reform (KPA).

Page 77– "Roundtable on Sustainable Palm Oil" — Fred Pearce (2008) "The Slippery Business of Palm Oil," *The Guardian*, Nov. 6.

Page 78– "…seven Canadian mining companies" — "Canadian Mining Mission to Indonesia," March 14, 2009, Government of Canada website <www.kbrisin-gapura.com/news_1403_2009_2.php?lang=eng>.

CHAPTER 5

Page 81– "*nagars*" — These are self-defined neighbourhoods which have names, local identity boundaries and some collective history.

Page 81– Kalpana Sharma (2000) Rediscovering Dharavi: Stories from Asia's Largest Slum, Penguin Books, India.

Page 85– "…stopped constructing employee housing" — Suketu Mehta (2004), *Maximum City, Bombay Lost and Found*, Vintage Books, New York.

Page 86– Mike Davis (2006) *Planet of Slums*, Verso, New York.

Page 86– The Bhabha Atomic Research Centre is modelled on the Chalk River nuclear facility in northern Ontario.

Page 90– "…benefit to the people was zero." — Lorna Kalaw-Tirol (2000) *Biography of Jockin Arputham*, for the Ramon Magsaysay Award for Peace and International Understanding.

Page 93– Arjun Appadurai (2002) "Deep Democracy: Urban Governamentality and the Horizon of Politics," *Public Culture*, 14, 1.

Page 95– David Satterthwaite (2001) "Reducing Urban Poverty: Constraints on the Effectiveness of Aid Agencies and Development Banks and Some Suggestions for Change," *Environment and Urbanization*, 13, 1.

Page 96– "Average people in affluent nations" — A 2007 Canadian Defence and Foreign Affairs Institute survey found that 70 percent of Canadians agreed with the statement that Canada has a moral obligation to help poor countries, and 13 percent disagreed (from Stephen Brown "CIDA under the Gun," in *Canada Among Nations 2007: What Room for Manoeuvre?* Jean Daudelin and Daniel Schwanen eds., (2008) McGill-Queens University Press, Montreal).

Page 96– "real aid stood at only $42 billion" — from *Real Aid: Making Technical Assistance Work* (2005) ActionAid International, London. The questionable use of so much overseas development aid money stands in stark contrast to the remittance payments sent home by those who manage to immigrate legally or — increasingly — illegally to rich nations often to work in shadowy and exploitative job environments. These sums now constitute ever higher percentages of poor-country GDP: from about one-tenth in countries such as Guatemala, the Dominican Republic, Bangladesh, Uganda and Sri Lanka, to more than 20 percent in Haiti, Lebanon, Lesotho and Guyana. In Honduras, it is 26 percent, according to World Bank 2006 data. Overall, an estimated $240 billion in remittance flows went to developing countries, not counting the considerable amounts of cash sent back through informal channels. This money goes directly to poor families and is spent in local economies.

Page 97– Pekka Hirvonen (2005) "Stingy Samaritans: Why Recent Increases in Development Aid Fail to Help the Poor," *Global Policy Forum*, New York.

Page 97– "foreign assistance was tied" — from the Center for Global Development.

Page 97– Canadian aid statistics from interview with David Tomlinson, Canadian Council for International Cooperation, and Brown, "CIDA Under the Gun."

Page 97– "aggregate figures…" — interview with Stephen Brown.

Page 98– "asset-based community development" — Oxfam Canada has been using ABCD in Ethiopia since 2003. So far, villages in three different regions have found solutions to their problems using quite minimal amounts of external funding and lots of local initiative. This has brought about several knock-on effects, including greater respect for women and higher numbers of girls in school. Oxfam has been supported in this new method by St. Francis Xavier University's Coady Institute. See "The Road to Self-Reliance: ABCD," by Lucie Goulet (2008) in *From Poverty to Power*, Oxfam International.

Page 99– Dirk-Jan Koch et al. (2008) " Keeping a Low Profile: What Determines the Allocation of Aid by Non-Governmental Organizations?" Kiel Working Paper 1406, Kiel Institute for the World Economy, Kiel, Germany.

Page 99– "…tended to cluster" — Working in similar areas on similar projects does not, however, translate into cooperation. See Real Aid, Op. Cit.

Page 99– Paul Collier (2007), *The Bottom Billion: Why the Poorest Countries Are Failing and What Can Be Done About It*, Oxford University Press, New York.

Page 100– "radical pragmatism" — Mark Swilling, "Hear the Forest Grow."

CHAPTER 6

Page 107– "…same place the following day." — Of this event, Sheela Patel has written: "We would readily have embraced a strategy of resistance but for our commitment to explore solutions jointly. And the women had clearly indicated their preferred strategy of negotiating rather than fighting." Sheela Patel (2007) *Reflections on Innovation, Assessment and Social Change: A SPARC Case Study*. Produced for the Assessing Social Change Initiative.

Page 108– "the market-led development approach…" — In that sense, it is somewhat similar to market-led agrarian reform initiatives, which put forward voluntary sales of farmland by willing landlords to individual peasants, rather than ex-propriations based on social pressure.

Page 108– Jason Cons and Kasia Paprocki (2008) "The Limits of Microcredit: A Bangladesh Case" in *Food First Backgrounder*, 14, 4. See also Lamia Karim (2008) in "Demystifying Micro-credit: The Grameen Bank, NGOs and Neoliberalism in Bangladesh," *Cultural Dynamics*, 20, 1, where the author examines "how Bangladeshi rural women's honor and shame are instrumentally appropriated by micro-credit NGOs in the furtherance of their capitalist interests"; and "Wealth and Controversy in Microlending," *New York Times*, July 30, 2010.

Page 109– Arjun Appadurai, "Deep Democracy."

Page 109– "…adaptable dynamics" — Swilling, "Hear the Forest Grow."

Page 112– "loans from local banks" — A major guarantor of such loans is Coventry, U.K.-based Homeless International, which has been working with the Indian Alliance for twenty years.

Page 114– Swilling, "Hear the Forest Grow."

Page 114– "human resource transfers" — interview with David Tomlinson.

Page 114– "consultants don't come cheap" — In another notorious case, the UK's Department of International Development, the Asian Development Bank and the World Bank spent $100 million on consultants to advise the state govern-ment of Orissa on how to privatize its electricity services. For more scandalous examples, see *Profiting from Poverty: Privatisation Consultants, DFID and Public Services* by John Hilary, a War on Want report published in 2004.

Page 115– The Commission on International Development was sponsored by the International Bank for Reconstruction and Development, better known now as the World Bank, and Pearson served as its chair from 1968–69.

CHAPTER 7

Page 121– *cartoneando*, from *cartón*, the Spanish word for cardboard.

Page 122– Siderar is a subsidiary of the Italian multinational Grupo Techint.

Page 123– Peter Ranis, "Argentina's Worker-Occupied Factories and Enterprises."

Page 124– "living below the poverty line" — the stats on poverty are from a variety of sources including Esteban Magnani (2009) *The Silent Change: Recovered Businesses in Argentina*, Editorial Teseo, Buenos Aires. Esteban, a key member of the crew for the 2004 Canadian documentary, *The Take*, currently works at worker micro-finance organization La Base.

Page 125– "…out of touch with people's needs" — Hannah Baldock (2002) "Child Hunger Deaths Shock Argentina," *The Guardian*, November 25.

Page 125– "…had resorted to it by 2002." — Jessica Koehs, cited in César Rodríguez Garavito (2006) "Solidarity Economy and the Struggle for Social Citizenship in Times of Globalization," in *Another Production Is Possible*.

Page 125– James Petras (2003) "Argentina: 18 Months of Popular Struggle: A Balance" available from <http://petras.lahaine.org/articulo. php?p=1669&more=1&c=1>.

Page 125– Andrés Ruggeri (2006) "The Worker-Recovered Enterprises in Argentina: The Political and Socioeconomic Challenges of Self-Management," translated by Marcelo Vieta. Paper presented at Another World Is Necessary: Center for Global Justice Annual Workshop.

Page 125– Supported by the University of Buenos Aires' Open Faculty Program, the Centre for Documentation of Recuperated Businesses (CDRB) is based inside the Chillavert workers-run printing factory.

Page 126– An early member of the MNFRT, Union y Fuerza became extremely successful, increasing production and hiring workers to the point where its cooperative decided to hire a consultant to manage production, and leave the movement. Soon it began to encounter severe economic problems, and by May 2009, a number of workers approached Luis Caro for advice.

Page 126– Zanón, which is not a member of any movement, was finally expropriated in September 2009.

Page 128– "…even oppose the workers" — Julian Rebón and Ignacio Saavedra (2006). "Empresas Recuperadas: La Autogestion de los Trabajadores," Capital Intellectual, Buenos Aires. This has not always been the case in factories recuperated by their workers in other countries and contexts. Since 1991, various trade unions have encouraged and advised the workers of failing enterprises in taking over and managing them themselves. Currently, Brazil's National Association of Workers in Self-managed and Profit-sharing Enterprises represents fifty-two factories run by workers out of 307 worker-managed cooperative projects. In Kolkata, the Left Front government of West Bengal state and the Centre for Indian Trade Unions also supported the formation of workers' cooperatives in response to factory closings throughout the 1980s, eighteen of which exist today.

Page 128– José Abelli is a union leader, lawyer and activist from the city of Rosario, and is now president of FACTA. Eduardo Murúa was a *montonero* militant in the late 1980s. He became a deputy in the Province of Buenos Aires legislature in 2003.

CHAPTER 8

Page 136– Néstor Kirchner died of a heart attack on October 23, 2010.

Page 136– "…working class in general." See Committee for a Workers International, December 2001; Tony Saunois (2002) in *Socialism Today*, 62, Feb,; and James Petras in ISR, interview. According to Andrés Ruggeri: "No popular organization or movement proposing fundamental changes to the social and economic structure of Argentina could take advantage of the scenario. And while it is also true that the insurrection helped put the brakes on the exorable journey to ruin the old Argentina was on, it did not, nor did it know how to, lay the foundations for constructing a new society."

Page 137– "...taking home salaries" — The legal minimum salary in 2009 was 1240 pesos per month.

Page 141– La Base/Working World was founded when Bradley Martin approached Canadian film makers Avi Lewis and Naomi Klein at a New York screening of their documentary *The Take* to talk about setting up micro-finance schemes for worker-occupied cooperatives in Argentina. By summer of 2009, it had made 177 loans totalling 2 million pesos to fifty-three cooperatives. Thanks to its flexible repayment schemes, the Arrufat chocolate factory, for example, was able to take advantage of demand over Easter and augment the production of chocolate eggs. For Martin, this kind of financing provides not only resources but also partnership.

Page 142– Julian Rebón (2004) *Desobedeciendo al Desempleo: La experiencia de las empresas recuperadas*, Picaso-La Rosa Blindada, Buenos Aires.

Page 143– "oceans of debt..." — According to *The Guardian*'s Paddy Allen, at one point the notional value of all debt-based derivatives reached $863 trillion, "many times the value of all the economic activity on the planet."

Page 144– *Pagina 12*, "Empresas Recuperadas con la Ley a Favor," August 20, 2010.

CONCLUSION

Page 148– Ela Bhatt (2006) *We Are So Poor But So Many: The Story of Self-Employed Women in India*, Oxford University Press.

Page 148– "establish a parliament." — Readers might recall a news item in 2006 about a triple murder at the royal palace in Kathmandu that left the Nepali king, queen and crown prince dead. The late king's brother, Gyandendra, took over and dismissed the nation's congress before being ousted himself a year later by a popular uprising.

Page 149– Hemant Ojha and Netra Timsina (2007) "From Grassroots to Policy Deliberation," in *Knowledge Systems and Natural Resources: Management, Policy and Institutions in Nepal*, Hemant Ojha et al., eds, Foundation Books, Delhi.

Page 150– Bruce Missingham (2004) *The Assembly of the Poor in Thailand: From Local Struggles to National Protest Movement*, University of Washington Press, Seattle.

Page 150– Bruce Missingham (2011) "The Pak Mun Dam: Social Conflict and Community Organizing" in *Transcending State Boundaries: Modernity, Cultural Meaning and Identity in the Mekong Region*, Chayan Vaddhanaphuti and Amporn Jirattikorn, eds. Chang Mai University, Chang Mai, Thailand.

Page 151– Abahlali baseMdojono has been at loggerheads for many years with the SDI over their differing strategies and what the former considered selling out to the same government bodies that visit such violence on the poor. The two groups do cooperate, however, on some initiatives.

Page 151– GAVO — Duncan Green (2009) *From Poverty to Power*, Oxfam International, London.

Page 152– The UGPM is a member of Senegal's Conseil National de Concertacion et Coopération des Ruraux, which in turn is a member of La Vía Campesina.

Page 153– Srilatha Batliwala, *Grassroots Movements as Transnational Actors*.

Acknowledgements

Aside from those interviewed, the generous assistance of many others was crucial to the research I undertook for this book. For their exact and patient interpreting skills I would like to thank Adi Bramasto in Indonesia, and Maria Lobo and Sharmila Ginonkhar in India. Three wonderful women, Neelam Kshirsagar, Fatou Diop and Dolores Gallichio, provided me with a home away from home in Mumbai, Dakar and Buenos Aires respectively.

I am also grateful to Anna Maria Straube and Cassia Bechara in Brazil, Aly Cisse of the International Labour Organization office in Dakar, Tejo Pramono of La Vía Campesina in Jakarta and professor Alan Sears, who gave me valuable advice for this book. My sister Mary Dwyer took care of emergencies and problems for me while I was away, and my husband Luis Porter encouraged and supported me in this endeavour.

I would also like to thank the Canada Council for the Arts and the Ontario Arts Council for grants that helped make the research and writing of this book possible.

Index

Abahlali baseMdojono, 151, 163.
Abelli, José, 128, 162.
Aceh, 65, 77.
ActionAid, 96, 115, 160.
adat, 50-51.
African National Congress, 37, 152.
agrarian reform, 10, 19, 22, 25, 38-9, 41, 44, 46, 51, 54, 63-65, 70, 74, 156, 157, 159, 161.
agribusiness, 2, 5, 8, 10, 36-8, 44, 76, 157.
agro-ecology, 32, 36.
Amazon, 17, 19, 21, 33, 37, 40, 56, 157, 158, 159.
Appadurai, Arjun, 93, 101, 109, 111, 115, 159, 161.
Aquino, José Alberto, 141
Aracruz Celulose S.A., 37-9, 157.
Araguaia, 19, 33, 157
Archer Daniels Midland, 36, 157.
Arputham, Joachim 'Jockin', 88, 159.
Asian Economic Crisis of 1997-98, 66.
Assembly of the Poor, 57, 149-150, 154,

Bakrie Group, 71.
Banten, 59-62, 69, 71.
Basic Agrarian Law, 51, 65, 68, 159.
Batliwala, Srilatha, 8, 153-4, 155, 163.
Beck, Scott, 41-2, 151.
Bendang, Sukardi, 74.
Benn, Tony, 12, 155.
Berton, Eleonora, 133, 143.
Bhabha Atomic Research Centre, 86, 159.
Bharatiya Janata Party, 84.

Bhatt, Ela, 147-8, 163.
Bio-fuels, 36, 77.
Branford, Sue, 20, 40, 156, 157, 158.
Bras, Roberto, 25.
Brazil,
  and military dictatorship, 16, 21, 33,
  and land distribution, 10, 17-21, 36-7, 40-6, 78, 90-1, 156, 158,
Borras, Saturnino, 37, 156, 157.
Burra, Sundar, 100.
Bush, George W., 37.
Brown, Stephen, 98, 115, 160.
Brukman suit factory, 130, 140, 142.

Camargo, Antonio 32-4, 39, 44.
Canadian Council for International Cooperation (CCIC), 97.
Canadian International Development Agency (CIDA), 97, 98, 160.
Canadian International Development Research Centre (IDRC), 52.
Cardoso, Bethania, 26-8, 31.
Cardoso, Fernando Henrique, 22, 34, 158.
Cargill, 36, 157.
Caro, Luis, 123, 127-135, 139-140, 142-3, 162.
Casaldáliga, Dom Pedro, 19, 141.
Catholic Church, 17, 23, 31, 57, 156.
Community-Based Forest Management, 62-3, 159.
Central Java Peasants Union, 70.
Centre for the Documentation of Recuperated Businesses (CDRB), 125, 127, 136, 145, 162.

165

Central Unica dos Trabalhadores
  (CUT), 56.
Cibaliung, 59-62, 159.
Collective for the Support of Local
  Development (CADEL), 152.
Collier, Paul, 99, 160.
Communist Party of Indonesia (PKI),
  65-6.
community police stations, 87.
Cons, Jason, 108, 161.
Conservation International, 55.
Congress Party, 84.
cooperatives, 12, 18, 21, 44-5,
  Argentina, 7, 10, 122, 126-146, 162,
    163.
  Brazil, 5, 162.
  farming, 27.
  India, 101, 162.
  Indonesia, 75.
  Java, 45.
  self-management, 7.
Cuba, 18, 28, 129.
Confederation of Indigenous
  Nationalities of Ecuador
  (CONAIE), 41-2, 151.
Confederation of Agrarian Reform
  Cooperatives (CONCRAB), 44-5.
Coronel, Alejandro, 122, 128, 144,
  146.

Da Silva, Luiz Inácio 'Lula', 22, 37-42,
  158.
Da Silva, Paulo Barros, 15, 18, 31,
  45-6, 59.
Davis, Mike, 86, 159.
De Carvalho, Horácio Martins, 20-1,
  156.
De la Rúa, Fernando, 122, 125, 127.
De Oliveira, Jose Batista, 29, 36, 45.
De Souza, Rubinilsa Leandro, 9, 19,
  22, 30-1.
Boaventura de Souza Santos, 143, 156.
Dharavi, 81-4, 88, 92, 101, 111, 159.
Di Gregorio, Monica, 51, 158.
Dowie, Mark, 55-6, 58, 158.
Dutch East India Company, 59.

East Timor, 65.
Ecological Research Institute (IPE), 35.
Ecuador, 41, 145.
Efendi, Rustam, 72, 78.
Espiritu Santo, 21, 33-4, 38-9.
Ethiopia, 38, 86, 155, 160.
eucalyptus, 19, 33, 35-9, 41, 58, 150.
Ezrah Jewish Association for Welfare
  and Mutual Aid, 132.
extractive reserves, 56.

Federation of Community Forest Users
  (FECOFUN), 148-9.
First Nations, 154.
food dumping, 76, 157.
Forest Peasants Group, 54.
framing, 6, 57, 142.
Freire, Paulo, 1, 18, 25, 30, 68.

Geisler, Charles, 55.
General Assistance and Volunteer
  Organization (GAVO), 151, 163.
George, Diana, 122, 137-9, 142.
Ghandi, Indira, 90.
Ghandi, Mahatma, 147.
Ginonkhar, Sharmila, 92.
Goffman, Erving, 6, 155.
Grameen Bank, 107-9, 161.
Grassroots Social Movements, 2, 3-4,
  6, 8, 11, 17-18, 20-1, 39-43, 66,
  78, 91, 147-8, 154, 155, 156. 163.
  and violence against, 70-1, 148,
    163.
Guarani, 38-9.
Guatemala, 37, 160.
Guevara, Ernesto, 'Che', 25, 28.
Gutiérrez, Lucio, 41-2.
Grissinopolis, 128, 136.

Haiti, 160.
Haryanto, Kito, 49, 63.
Hauser Center for Nonprofit
  Organizations, 8, 153.
Hirvonen, Pekka, 97, 114, 160.
Honduras, 37-8, 160.
Hospital Israelita, 131-5, 141-3.